A Concise Grammar
for English Language Teachers

Tony Penston

 TP Publications

Introduction

This book is in fact the new edition of *A Grammar Course for TEFL Certificate*. The change of title is to reflect a completely revamped work and serve a wider readership.

The commendations for the first edition have justified my main objectives: to present the essentials of tesol grammar in a concise and user-friendly way, making them comprehensible in a short period and easily locatable during lesson planning.

Like the first edition, this book has been written mainly for participants on a teacher training course, but with the increase in content it should also serve well as a reference for practising teachers. It presupposes a native-speaker or near native-speaker level of competence in English, but takes nothing for granted regarding the reader's knowledge of grammar. It gets straight to the point, knowing what the teacher needs and not wasting space with what they don't.

I am cognizant of the value of coursebooks and recommend their use to varying degrees, hence the many extracts from coursebooks in this publication. But besides the coursebook there is a growing popularity of the use of authentic materials, games, instant lessons, etc, so the teacher now has to operate with more unpredictable language in the classroom. Today's language learner is sophisticated and demands both communicative activities *and* competent grammar explanation.

Where the matching tasks in this book are used in tutorials the tutor should cut out and mount/laminate the sections for group/pair work where possible. The tutor may also project the task/answer. Copyright is waived for such tutor activities but I would stress that no further copying is allowed under copyright legislation and it is strongly recommended that *each course participant should have a copy of this book.*

It must be stressed that the activities in this book are designed for *teachers*, not for language *learners*. The extracts from ELT coursebooks and the Teaching Notes are intended to show the difference between what the teacher should know and what and how they should teach.

I would here like to include a few points on what I believe an English language teacher should know about grammar and its teaching:

1. The teacher should know **the terminology**, because it is very difficult to explain a grammar rule without knowing the names of the items affected by that rule.

2. The teacher should know **the structure rules**, simply because most learners are comparing those of English with their own while they learn, and clear explanation should be available to the student on request.

3. The teacher should know **how to fit the semantic (meaning) with the grammatical**, i.e. we don't just explain the *what* of the structure, but also the *why*, the use/function of the structure. The good teacher knows how to teach the 'feeling' for the language besides the structure of it.

4. The teacher should know **when to teach grammar**, better said, *exploit* grammar to aid the learning of the language. This involves knowing whether their students are the type who use grammar as a 'mental framework' for language acquisition (this sounds abstract but this type is evidenced by constant questioning about grammatical points, often consequently drawing accusations of testing the teacher). It also involves waiting till learners become curious about a grammar point and being able to present a grammar lesson on that.

5. The teacher should know **when not to teach grammar**, that is, not to present grammar for grammar's sake. Primarily the teacher is a teacher of English communication, not of English grammar, and these in effect are two different subjects. Native speakers never had to learn (consciously) the grammar of their own language in order to communicate.

6. The teacher should know **how much grammar to teach at each level**. Most experienced teachers know when to tell a white lie in order to keep information simple and not overwhelm slow learners or learners at lower levels.

This book should go some way towards providing the skills outlined in the points above. Remarks and suggestions from users of this book would be greatly appreciated.

A note on the layout: as far as possible paragraphing has been subject to visual neatness with an end to easier learning – few paragraphs are broken across pages, for example. As a consequence paragraph numbering and content may seem a little incoherent or imbalanced. I apologise for any distraction that this may cause.

Contents

Abbreviations

adj. adv.	adjective adverb	pref.	preferred / preferred with
AmE	American English (northern/general)	prep.	preposition
aux.	auxiliary verb	pro.	pronoun
BrE	British English	sbdy	somebody
coll.	colloquial (spoken) use mainly	SUBJ	subject
def/indef. art.	definite/indefinite article	T	task/teacher
det./DET.	determiner	TEF/SL	Teaching English as a Foreign/
ELT	English Language Teaching		Second Language
IrE	Irish English	TESOL	Teaching English to Speakers of
L1	first/native language, mother tongue		Other Languages
L2	second/foreign/target language	verb/-phrase	verb or verb phrase
noun/-phrase	noun or noun phrase		

Symbols

*	Asterisk at start of sentence indicates it is ungrammatical (unacceptable).
?	Question mark at start of sentence/word indicates it is semantically obscure or not fully acceptable.
( )° ... ( )°	Only one of the parenthesized items may occur in the sentence.
≈	Similar in meaning or usage.
=	Synonymous with
~	Compare with

1 The simple sentence and its parts

1.1 Subject, verb, object

A tree diagram (branching downwards) serves well to show the constituents of a sentence:

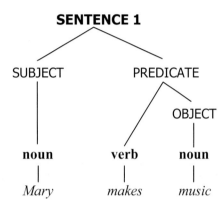

SENTENCE 1

Sentence 1 shows us that a sentence must have two main branches: the SUBJECT and the PREDICATE. The subject is usually the 'doer', or the person/thing described. The predicate means 'the rest of the sentence' to put it crudely but simply.

The **verb** conveys an action or state. The OBJECT is the person/thing at the receiving end of the action, hence *music* is the object of the verb *makes*.

Noun, verb, noun (words in bold above and in future sentences) are the constituents called **word classes** or **parts of speech**. Words are classed according to their grammatical properties.

In every sentence there must be a **finite verb**, i.e. a verb with a tense. A verb can change its form to show tense, e.g. *make : made*. The verb in sentence 1 is in the present tense. Tenses are covered in the next three chapters.

SUBJECT:	the 'doer', or where there's no action, the person/thing considered.
PREDICATE:	the rest of the sentence after the subject.
verb:	conveys an action or state, e.g. *to carry, to be*.
OBJECT:	the person/thing at the receiving end of the action.
noun:	a person, place or thing, e.g. *Mary, Beijing, door*.
finite verb:	a verb with a tense.

In sentence 1 the subject and object are **nouns**. They could be **pronouns**: <u>She</u> makes <u>it</u>. Pronouns are dealt with in more detail in chapter 7.

pronoun:	a word standing for (pro) a noun, e.g. *he, they*.

Some sentences consist of only one word, e.g. the imperative *Stop!*, but then the missing part is understood and we can construct an 'underlying' sentence, in this case something like *You (will) stop!*

Subject-verb-object is logical to English speakers but it may not be the word order of your students' language. Allow time for mental re-formulation and provide lots of rich input (easy listening and reading, with unforced interactions) especially at lower levels, before expecting accurate production.

Teaching note 1.1

Task 1.1 Many words can function as nouns or verbs. Two words in the list below cannot serve this dual function. Which are they?

spoon	serve	husband	compost	rile	keep
meet	sloop	convict	effect	remove	rime

It is advisable to have a dictionary to hand when writing formal work, correcting homework, for use in class, <u>and</u> when using this book. Popular ELT dictionaries include the *Oxford Advanced Learner's Dictionary*, the *Macmillan English Dictionary for Advanced Learners* and similar from other ELT publishers.

Ask the publishers for class materials for use with their dictionaries.

Teaching note 1.2

1.2 Subject, verb

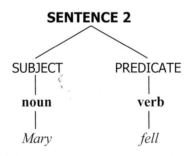

In sentence 2 there is no object. Mary didn't fall her body, didn't fall the clarinet, etc. The verb *to fall* can't take an object; it is an **intransitive verb**. Other intransitive verbs are *to cough, to hesitate,* etc.

In sentence 1 the verb *to make* <u>must</u> have an object. We can't just say *Mary makes;* our listener would say *Mary makes what?.* Verbs that must take an object are called **transitive verbs**. Other transitive verbs are *to have, to afford,* etc.

> **transitive verb:** a verb that must take an object.
>
> **intransitive verb:** a verb that cannot take an object.

Many verbs may be used transitively ... or ... intransitively:

> Mary sings ballads.   Mary sings.
> John walks the dog.   John walks.

1.3 Adjective, adverb

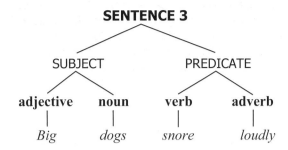

Sentence 3 reminds us that adjectives mostly come *before* the noun, and adverbs of manner often *follow* the verb (or verb + object). The syntax in **Dogs big loudly snore* may be okay in many languages but not in English (an asterisk at the start of a sentence signifies it is ungrammatical).

> **adjective:** a word that gives information about (modifies) a noun.
>
> **adverb of manner:** a word that gives information about (modifies) a verb.

1.4 The articles, modals, infinitive

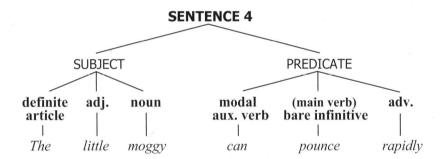

In sentence 4 we are introduced to **the definite article**, a **modal auxiliary verb** (shortened to *modal aux.*, *modal verb*, even simply *modal*) and **the infinitive**.

The citation form of verbs, e.g. *to swim, to afford, to snore*, is the infinitive, or to be more precise, **the infinitive with *to*** or **the full infinitive**.

Modal aux. verbs, e.g. *may, might, can, could, would*, etc, are followed by the **base form** of the **main verb**, more commonly called **the infinitive without *to*** or **the bare infinitive**.

The imperative (command/order) also uses the bare infinitive form of the verb, e.g. <u>Strike while the iron's hot.</u>

> **definite article:** *the*, indicating the known or unique.
>
> **indefinite article:** *a, an*, indicating the not known/the not unique/any one.
>
> **modal aux. verb:** *can, could, may, might, will, would, shall, should, must, ought to.* Modals indicate ability, possibility, permission, advice, deduction, etc. They are **followed by the bare infinitive.**
>
> **infinitive:** base form of the verb, usually with *to*. It has no tense.
>
> **main verb:** a verb which can occur on its own, or after one or more auxiliary verbs, whereupon it carries the most 'sense'. Sometimes called lexical verb.
>
> **finite verb (revised):** a verb with a tense, including modal aux. verbs, which although they carry the tense don't show tense marking (inflection).

Task 1.2 Draw a tree diagram for the sentence *A real man would shave closely*, using the term *bare infinitive* in the appropriate position.

Task 1.3 Explain the errors below in grammatical terms. (L1 = learner's native language)

1. **Health is like a jewel very precious.* (Italian L1)
2. **We have to respect some importants rules.* (Italian L1)
3. **... because their parents they didn't know how to bring them up.* (Arabic L1)
4. ** They laugh at it, but is not very funny.* (Spanish L1)

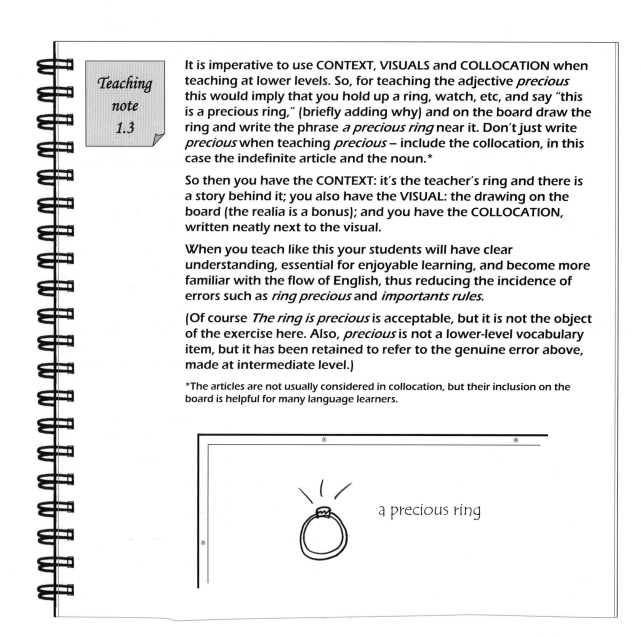

Teaching note 1.3

It is imperative to use CONTEXT, VISUALS and COLLOCATION when teaching at lower levels. So, for teaching the adjective *precious* this would imply that you hold up a ring, watch, etc, and say "this is a precious ring," (briefly adding why) and on the board draw the ring and write the phrase *a precious ring* near it. Don't just write *precious* when teaching *precious* – include the collocation, in this case the indefinite article and the noun.*

So then you have the CONTEXT: it's the teacher's ring and there is a story behind it; you also have the VISUAL: the drawing on the board (the realia is a bonus); and you have the COLLOCATION, written neatly next to the visual.

When you teach like this your students will have clear understanding, essential for enjoyable learning, and become more familiar with the flow of English, thus reducing the incidence of errors such as *ring precious* and *importants rules*.

(Of course *The ring is precious* is acceptable, but it is not the object of the exercise here. Also, *precious* is not a lower-level vocabulary item, but it has been retained to refer to the genuine error above, made at intermediate level.)

*The articles are not usually considered in collocation, but their inclusion on the board is helpful for many language learners.

a precious ring

1.4.1 The split infinitive

In *to boldly go*, the infinitive *to go* has been 'split' by the adverb *boldly*. This used to be considered 'bad grammar', the 'correct' form being *boldly to go* or *to go boldly*. However, the split infinitive is now generally acceptable, unless one desires to address formally one's audience.

1.5 'Be' as auxiliary verb, + -ing participle

In sentence 5 below we can see the indefinite article *a*, and the verb *be* (in the form of *was*) in its function of **primary auxiliary verb** (relax, there are only two types of aux. verb: modal and primary). In this instance the main verb takes the *-ing* form (pronounced 'ing' or I-N-G) and may be called the **-ing participle**. It used to be called the **present participle**, but this term is not user-friendly, having nothing to do with the present tense. Tenses are covered in the next three chapters.

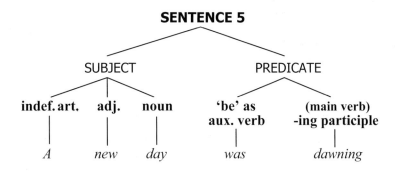

SENTENCE 5

	SUBJECT			PREDICATE	
indef. art.	adj.	noun	'be' as aux. verb	(main verb) -ing participle
A	*new*	*day*	*was*	*dawning*

> **primary aux. verb:** *be, have,* and *do. Be* and *have* are not followed by the bare infinitive. Primary aux. verbs can also act as main verbs.
> Forms of *be* are: *am, are, is, were, was, being* and *been.*
>
> **-ing participle:** form of main verb occurring after *be* to form continuous aspect of tenses (see chapter 2).

Task 1.4 Write the word class for each word in bold below as indicated by the example. If the verb follows an aux. verb there is no need to state 'main verb' just state what form the verb is in.

	WORD CLASS a)	WORD CLASS b)
0. *We reached **an** understanding.*	*pronoun*	*indefinite article*
1. ***Time** was **passing**.*		
2. *You **should** know **the** score.*		
3. *I **am** asking **them** to do it.*		
4. *Kiri can **sing** quite **beautifully**.*		
5. ***It** was a **rash** decision.*		
6. *Which **herd** was he **herding**?*		
7. *Mary **beheld** a **ghostly** scene.*		
8. *Jack said he **might** call by.*		
9. ***Shall** I **see** who it is?*		
10. *A child could **easily** do this.*		

1.6 Pronoun, preposition

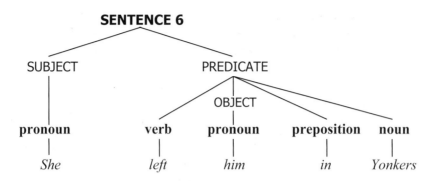

SENTENCE 6

SUBJECT   PREDICATE

OBJECT

pronoun   **verb**   **pronoun**   **preposition**   **noun**

She   *left*   *him*   *in*   *Yonkers*

In sentence 6 we are introduced to (personal) **pronouns** and **prepositions**. You may notice that personal pronouns are the only words in English that have a different form for subject and object, i.e. sentence 6 is not *She left he.*

Observe the paradigm of personal pronouns below (the pronoun *it* may not often have personal reference but is included to complete the usual set):

PERSONAL PRONOUNS

	SUBJECT		**OBJECT**	
	singular	**plural**	**singular**	**plural**
1st person	*I*	*we*	*me*	*us*
2nd person	*you*	*you*	*you*	*you*
3rd person	*he/she/it*	*they*	*him/her/it*	*them*

pronoun (revised):   a word which stands for a noun or noun phrase (see sentence 8) e.g. *he, it, them,* also indicating the communicators, *I, you, we.*

preposition: Many prepositions indicate location or direction, e.g. ***over*** *the moon,* ***to*** *the Louvre*; many others indicate time, e.g. ***in*** *July,* ***after*** *eight*; the rest are 'miscellaneous', e.g. ***for*** *me,* ***to*** *my surprise,* ***because of*** *him,* ***regarding*** *the divorce,* etc.
Areas of difficulty include their collocations with nouns (e.g. *picture* ***of***), adjectives (e.g. *sorry* ***about/for***), and verbs (e.g. *listen* ***to***, *charge him* ***with***).

Complete the sentences using the following adjectives + the correct preposition:

   afraid   **different**   **interested**   **proud**   **responsible**   **similar**   ~~sure~~

1 I think she's arriving this evening, but I'm not ....*sure of*.... that.
2 Your camera is .... mine, but it isn't exactly the same.
3 Don't worry. I'll look after you. There's nothing to be ....
4 I never watch the news on television. I'm not .... the news.
5 The editor is the person who is .... what appears in a newspaper.
6 Sarah is a keen gardener. She's very .... her garden and loves showing it to visitors.
7 I was surprised when I met Lisa for the first time. She was .... what I expected.

From *English Grammar in Use* by R. Murphy (CUP). Adjective + preposition collocations.

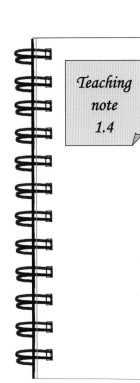

Teaching note 1.4

Coursebooks and resource books are a great help to teachers who don't have the time or the confidence to create their own materials. Indeed many schools stipulate the adherence to a specifed coursebook.

However, in some environments there may be a scarcity of resources and you should develop the skill of extending or developing what little there is available, and this includes using the students and yourself (and the board). In any case try not to be a slave to the photocopier, and reduce the time that your students spend looking down at their books or handouts. RELEVANT TOPICS, RELAXED INPUT and COMMUNICATIVE PRACTICE are the key to enjoyable teaching and learning.

The extract below from *Instant Lessons 1* demonstrates a communicative (free) practice activity for prepositions of time. The topic is relevant – it is about the student and their classmate – and the activity generates enjoyable practice in the form of individual and pair work. But the learning activity and fun need not end there – task 1.5 helps you exploit the idea for practising prepositions of place.

B Work individually to complete the questions. Then, in pairs, ask your questions and write down your partner's answers.

1 What did you do on … … … … … … … … … … … … …?

2 What are you going to do in … … … … … … … … … … … … … ?

3 What were you doing at … … … … … … … … … … … … …?

4 Are you going to see the match on … … … … … … … … … … … …?

5 Did you buy those clothes on … …   … … … … … … … … … … … …?

6 Where will you be in … … … … … … … … … … … … … ?

7 Who won the game on … … … … … … … … … … … …?

8 Did you go to the cinema on … … … … … … … … … … … … … ?

9 Did you stay at home at … … … … … … … … … … … …?

10 What did you do in … … … … … … … … … … … … …?

From *Instant Lessons 1* by D. Howard-Williams et al (Penguin). Prepositions of time – individual and pair work.

Task 1.5 Design an activity to practise prepositions of place, using the format of the excerpt above and pitching the language at elementary level. Use the same instructions, with the same number (10) of unfinished questions. Three have been done for you.

1. At night, do you leave your shoes under … … … … … … …?

2. Do you cook vegetables in … … … … … … … … … … …?

3. Are there any pictures on … … … … … … … … … … …?

1.7 Object case after preposition

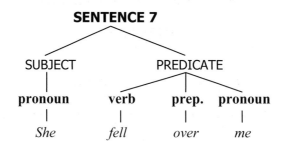

SENTENCE 7

SUBJECT   PREDICATE

pronoun   **verb**   **prep.**   **pronoun**

She   *fell*   *over*   *me*

Why is sentence 7 not *She fell over I?* Because as you can see **prepositions take the object case.** *Me* can't be the object of *fell,* because we know that *fall* is an intransitive verb. In a sentence such as *She sent him to me, him* is the object of the verb *send,* and *me* is the object of the preposition *to.*

a preposition(prep.)	is always followed by a noun, noun phrase (see 1.8) or pronoun in the object case (unless this has been moved out of normal position, e.g. *It was **me** she fell **over***).
case:	English has three cases: subject, object, and genitive (possessive). Case is usually defined as how a noun or pronoun changes depending on its position in a sentence. English nouns don't change their form for subject or object case.

1 Work with a partner. Complete the tables with an adverb or adjective from the stories on page 74.

Revenge is sweet			*Dinner by post*	
Adjective	**Adverb**		**Adjective**	**Adverb**
a) unhappy	*unhappily*		1 *different*	differently
b) ____	badly		2 early	____
c) ____	angrily		3 late	____
d) quick			4 ____	tidily
e) ____	beautifully		5 ____	attractively
f) careful	____		6 ____	well
g) quiet	____		7 loud	____

2 Work with a partner. Use the information in the tables in 1 to answer the questions on adverb formation.

   a) How do you make adverbs from most adjectives?
   b) How do you make adverbs from adjectives ending in *y*?
   c) What are the adverbs for the adjectives *good, early, late*?

From *Inside Out Elementary* by S. Kay & V. Jones (Macmillan). Adjective and adverb formation.

1.8 Noun phrase

Words cluster into phrases. Our next sentence shows two noun phrases.

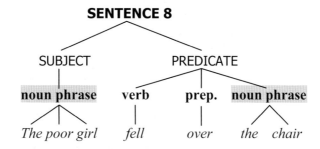

noun phrase:	a group of words made up of a noun and one or more words modifying or specifying it.
noun/-phrase:	a noun or noun phrase (convention used in this book).

1.9 Preposition phrase

This construction shows a preposition phrase. As you can see, phrases may be represented by triangles.

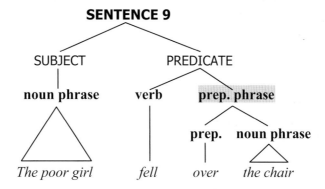

1.10 Adverbial

A preposition phrase usually functions as an adverb (in sentence 10, an adverb of place) and so is called an **adverbial** (see chapter 9, also for adverb phrase).

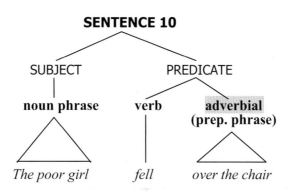

preposition phrase:	a group of words made up of a preposition and a following noun/phrase or pronoun. A type of **adverbial**.

One final phrase is the **verb phrase**. Grammarians interpret this as anything from a single verb up to the entire predicate. For ELT it is better interpreted as the auxiliary verb(s) plus main verb. However, no further treatment is merited here *except* to warn against confusion with *phrasal verb* (chapter 14).

1.11 Gerund (-ing form)

And now, what is the subject of the next sentence?

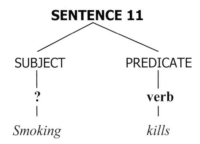

SENTENCE 11

SUBJECT	PREDICATE
?	**verb**
Smoking	*kills*

The word *smoking* is in subject position. We know that the subject of a sentence must contain a noun (or pronoun) so *smoking* here must be a noun of some sort.

Besides being the subject in a sentence, the word *smoking* can occupy other noun positions, e.g.

it can be the object of a verb: *She likes smoking;*
it can follow a preposition: *We put it down to smoking;*
it can be preceded by a definite article: *It's the smoking that does it.*

This noun that comes from a verb has long been called a **gerund**, sometimes **verbal noun**. Some modern grammars advocate the use of a more user-friendly term, e.g. **-ing form (used as a noun)**. However, *gerund* seems to hold its ground for various reasons.

> **gerund:** a word ending in *-ing*, derived from a verb and taking the place of a noun. Also known as **-ing form (used as a noun)**.

Task 1.6

Explain the error in
   *I look forward to see you.
Use the terms *preposition*, *gerund (or -ing form)* and *infinitive*.

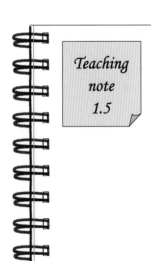

Teaching note 1.5

A fun way to revise vocabulary is to play 'X's and O's' on the board. One team is the X's and the other the O's. Write the first letter of the words you want to revise in the squares. Toss a coin for the first team to call a letter. Give a clue, and anyone can answer. The person to answer correctly calls the next letter. Write the answer under the letter for consolidation. Note how articles, plurals etc, can help distinguish the parts of speech.

C (to crown)	S₁ (soil)	T toes
E (easily)	M I might	X a loaf
S₂ to shave	B (between)	X deadly

The 'O' team have won above (the words in brackets are not shown yet, but are on the teacher's notes).

1.12 Linking verb

So far we have dealt only with verbs which convey or imply some activity. There is another type of verb worthy of attention:

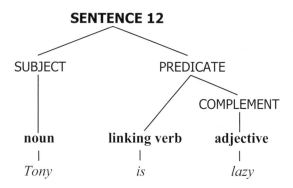

SENTENCE 12

In sentence 12 the verb *be* is used as a main verb (its other role is an aux. verb – see 1.5).

As we can see, this verb does not describe any activity; it just links a person or thing with a descriptor. It is therefore given the functional title **linking verb** (or *copula*) and is followed by the **subject complement**.

An **object complement** would occur after the object:

> *They elected <u>him</u>* (OBJECT) *<u>president</u>* (COMPLEMENT).

---

linking verb:	a verb that simply links the subject with what is being said about it. Linking verbs comprise *be* and verbs of appearance, sense, etc, e.g. *seem, feel, sound, become.* Also called *complement verb* or *copula.*
subject complement:	an adjective, noun/-phrase, pronoun or adverbial linked to the subject by a linking verb.

Task 1.7

The errors below are taken from the written work of intermediate level students. For each error,
  a) Re-write it correctly
  b) Explain it in grammatical terms.
  b) Comment on the student's L1 as a possible cause of the error.

The first one has been done for you.

0. *I like to see films in school auditorium.* (Chinese L1)
1. *I think I was member of this family.* (Japanese L1)
2. *The sports ground is in a town at the sea.* (Arabic L1)
3. *...I could feel the soft rain in my face.* (Spanish L1)
4. *I have never been in Mars.* (Spanish L1)
5. *I had to come back willinglessly.* (Chinese L1)
6. *I thought maybe I could found some animals there.* (Spanish L1)

0. a) *I like to see (the) films in <u>the</u> school auditorium.*
   b) *Omission of definite article where unique or known reference requires it.*
   c) *Perhaps there are no articles in the student's L1 and the student hasn't grasped the usage of the definite article in English.*

Note: what the student intended to say was gleaned from their written work. Please presume the more common intention, i.e. not *in school auditoriums/ia* above.

Teaching note 1.6

'Running through' an exercise list

Most grammar exercises involve filling in blanks. But how do you run through them in class? A popular routine is first to allow students to do them in pairs and then to check around, nominating one by one. But there's more to it than that, as observations of experienced teachers show. There is no perfect way, but some pointers are:

1) Briefly 'sell' the exercise by telling students how important it is to be able to use the structure being practised (state some benefits, give a couple of examples, use the board).

2) Give instructions audibly and succinctly, showing the page, pointing to the heading and checking that all students are following. You could ask a student to read the instructions.

3) If the first sentence is already done as an example, still have a good student read it aloud. This gives more time for the slower ones to understand what's required. If the first sentence is not done, do it yourself (with a good student) by way of example.

4) Initiate the collaborative pairwork. If some students prefer to work on their own that's fine.

5) During the pairwork make yourself available especially to the weaker students, passing an eye over their work to make sure they are on the right track (some teachers also have a brief chat with stronger pairs to allow the slower ones to catch up). If everything is going smoothly then sit down and relax – you deserve a rest.

6) Start the check-around when most of the students are finished. The slower ones will understand that the whole class can't always wait on them; be sure to help them when you come to the blanks that they haven't had time to fill in. Start with a good student.

7) Usually students should read out the full sentence to get pronunciation practice, not just say the missing word.

8) Nominate with respect and clarity – call out the number of the next sentence and ask the next student, by name, to attempt it, thanking them for any reasonable effort.

9) When you get a wrong answer don't just say "no" – thank the student by name and ask if anybody got a different answer. Confirm or correct the peer correction, loudly and clearly, then once more repeat the number and the correct answer.

10) Check that students have finished writing corrections before you call the next number.

11) If an exercise involves a two-part dialogue, even of just two lines, have two students read it.

12) Use your personality regarding the style of chit-chat and encouragement that should arise along the way. Remember, if it were just a case of saying "next ... right ... next ... wrong," etc, then a computer would be better. But you can do what a computer can't – encourage, cajole, involve, elicit comments.

13) When you've 'done' the section ask students to close their books, then review in a personalising style, i.e. elicit and feed the same structures but with relevant topics. This will not be possible with all exercises or all classes but it affords invaluable practice. It will also give you good training in getting students' heads out of the book. Don't forget to try a written extension activity also.

For the next task one of the course participants could be the 'teacher' and go through the list in the manner suggested above. The other participants could assess – in a friendly way – the application of the points (points 1, 5, 7, 11, 12, 13 will not apply in this context).

Task 1.8 Write the word class for each word in bold below as in the example. No phrases (noun or prep. phrases/adverbials) are included. There are three linking verbs.

	WORD CLASS a)	WORD CLASS b)
0. *We* reached *an* understanding.	*pronoun*	*indefinite article*
1. *I* **am** rolling **in** it.		
2. **Boots** are for **walking**.		
3. They **were** looking at **us**.		
4. She **seems** very **well** to me.		
5. **The** proof of the pudding is in the **eating**.		
6. I **will** be **seeing** you.		
7. I will **be** a monkey's **uncle**.		
8. **Stealthily** the fox approached the **old** barn.		
9. You **are** certainly **amongst** friends.		
10. If it's ok with **them** I'll **do** it.		

1.13 Indirect object

Many verbs can or must take two objects. The indirect object is usually a person, and when it follows the direct object it is preceded by the preposition *to* or *for*:

	SUBJECT	VERB	DIRECT OBJECT	INDIRECT OBJECT			SUBJECT	VERB	INDIRECT OBJECT	DIRECT OBJECT
1a	*Eve*	*gave*	*the apple*	*to Adam*	≈ 1b		*Eve*	*gave*	*Adam*	*the apple*
2a	*David*	*bought*	*a poodle*	*for you*	≈ 2b		*David*	*bought*	*you*	*a poodle*
3a	*David*	*bought*	*one/it*	*for you*	≈ 3b		*David*	*bought*	*you*	*one/(?it)*

The choice of which object comes first usually follows a general rule: **given/known information comes first, new information comes last.** For example in 1a we have been talking about the apple and so the new information *to Adam* comes last. In 1b we have been talking about Adam so *the apple* comes last (the article would normally be indefinite (*an* apple) but this apple is not so 'new').

This rule, usually called 'topic fronting', is not always applicable of course: the choice of *I bought one for you* over *I bought you one* may be governed by many factors, emphasis being a main one (as 3b shows, personal pronouns are not fully acceptable in end position).

Another factor governing order is **end-weight**, whereby longer clauses tend to be moved to the end of a sentence, e.g. *He bought each of his fair-skinned outdoor workers complaining of sunburn a hat* sounds cumbersome, so *He bought a hat for each of ...* would be preferred.

More examples of these verbs are:
> (with *to*) *feed, hand, leave, lend, pass, sell, show, teach.*
> (with *for*) *build, cook, find, keep, leave, play, pour, sing.*

Some ditransitive verbs, as these are called, may not allow transposition of their objects. These comprise mainly *explain, suggest, describe, indicate*:

4a	He	explained	the word	to me

≈

4b	He	explained	~~me~~	the word

He explained <u>to me</u> + DIRECT OBJECT is acceptable where emphasis is required, or more usually where the direct object is long (see reference to end-weight above).

1.14 Verb + object + preposition phrase

This is another type of ditransitive verb. It merits mention here because students invariably have difficulty in remembering the correct following preposition:

accuse sbdy **of**   deprive sbdy **of**
charge sbdy **with**   prevent sbdy **from**
congratulate sbdy **on**   sentence sbdy **to**

1.15 A note on tree diagrams

Tree diagrams are used by most syntacticians to show the phrase structure of sentences, but there is not general conformity on the branching or applications. I have in this chapter compromised between traditional and modern terminology in order to present the material in a user-friendly way for English language teachers.

The division of a sentence into only two major constituents, subject and predicate, is not sacrosanct. In the case of adverbials (see chapter 9) which are not tied to the verb phrase and commonly occur at the start or end of the sentence, there seems to be a strong case for a third major branch. Indeed, we can say that a sentence is composed of up to five major constituents: SUBJECT, VERB/-PHRASE, OBJECT, COMPLEMENT and ADVERBIAL.

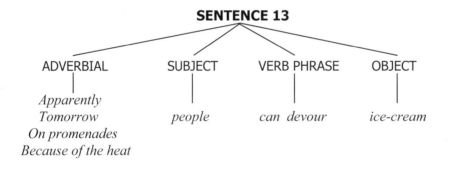

SENTENCE 13

ADVERBIAL	SUBJECT	VERB PHRASE	OBJECT
Apparently *Tomorrow* *On promenades* *Because of the heat*	*people*	*can devour*	*ice-cream*

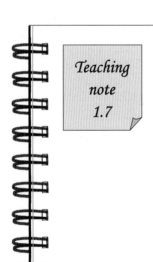

Teaching note 1.7

Experience tells us that students with an Indo-European L1 have little difficulty in coping with the syntax of English. However, the case is often different for others. Japanese students, for example, who are experiencing difficulty in correctly ordering constituent phrases or in conjoining clauses should benefit from the visual assistance the tree diagram provides.

However, as I reiterate throughout this book, IF THEY KNOW IT, DON'T TEACH IT, which means in this case if your students are able to communicate in reasonably well-structured sentences, or to acquire the rules of English sentence structure through normal communicative methodology then there's no need at all to teach sentence structure overtly.

And may I remind you that the material in this book is written for teachers, not for language learners. Please read the introduction for details.

2 Verb tenses 1:
Present simple and continuous
Past simple and continuous
Future simple and continuous

2.1 Present, past and future tenses

There are 3 tenses in English - **present**
past
future

Each of these can be expanded to include certain aspects, as we shall see later.

Our initial look at tenses will consist of a short story. First, just read the story slowly. At this first reading there is no need to learn the titles of the tenses in parentheses - just look and move on.

TENSE SITUATIONS – PART I

She is teaching.

Sue is a photographer. She **takes** (PRESENT SIMPLE) photos of famous people for a lifestyle magazine.
But at the moment she **is taking** (PRESENT CONTINUOUS) a course in English Language Teaching.

Sue remembers her first professional assignment. It was in 2003, and her tripod **broke** (PAST SIMPLE) as she **was taking** (PAST CONTINUOUS) a photo of the Sultan of Brunei.

Sue has a grammar 'test' tomorrow morning. She is a little anxious but her colleagues say she **will sail** (FUTURE SIMPLE) through it.
She **will be presenting** (FUTURE CONTINUOUS) a lesson on the past simple and continuous, based on a text about the moon landing in 1969
(… *as he was stepping onto the moon* … etc.).

Part 1 of *Tense Situations* introduces us to the three basic English tenses: PRESENT, PAST and FUTURE.

Note the third person singular -*s* ending in the present simple:

(1st person) *I*   *take*
(2nd person) *you*   *take*
(3rd person) *he/she/it*   *takes*

This is an oddity and may not be acquired easily. Allow for slips, include activities which elicit the third person singular (e.g. the 20 questions game 'What's his/her job?', the guessing game 'Who is this famous person?' etc.), use soft correction and time will look after the rest.

The table below lists the three basic tenses, PRESENT, PAST and FUTURE, each with SIMPLE and CONTINUOUS aspect (see 2.4), and includes an example and brief statement of the use of each. Please note that the uses here are very restricted for neatness' sake but are expanded later. For the 'going to' future, *shall* and other uses of *will* see chapter 4.

TENSE	EXAMPLE	USE
present simple	*She **takes** photos.*	regular/habitual event; fact; job
present continuous	*She **is taking** a course.*	happening now (temporary)
past simple	*Her tripod **broke**.*	completed past event
past continuous	*She **was taking** a photo.*	'simultaneous' past event
future simple	*She **will sail** through her test.*	prediction of completed event
future continuous	*She **will be presenting** a lesson.*	prediction of 'simultaneous' event / happening as a matter of course.

Focus

1 Before you read. The blockbuster film *Titanic*, told of the tragic events of April 14th 1912, when the luxury liner hit an iceberg and sank, killing 1,523 people.

Read about it

2 How did the disaster happen? Read the text and note down three events which contributed to the tragedy.

Countdown to tragedy

Sunday 14th April
Morning

The *Titanic* was sailing from Southampton to New York. It was the fourth day of her maiden voyage. Bruce Ismay of the White Star Line, the ship's owners, was sailing on the ship. Ismay wanted to arrive in New York a day early and he asked the Captain to increase the ship's speed. The Captain was unhappy, but he agreed. The ship's speed was increased to 21.5 knots.

9.40 pm

The *Titanic*'s wireless operator was working alone, when he received a message from another ship, the *Mesaba*, warning of icebergs in the area. The operator was busy sending and receiving passengers' messages and he did not pass the *Mesaba*'s warning to the Captain.

11.00 pm

It was a cold, moonless night. The lookouts were keeping watch, but they weren't using binoculars - the ship's pair were missing.

The first and second-class passengers were relaxing after dinner. The Captain was not on the bridge. He was getting ready for bed in his cabin.

11.37 pm

The two lookouts spotted a huge iceberg. It was about 500 metres in front of the *Titanic*. They telephoned the bridge with the message: 'Iceberg dead ahead.' The Quartermaster spun the ship's wheel as fast as he could. But it was too late. The ship was sailing too fast, and was too big to change direction quickly.

11.40 pm

The *Titanic* hit the iceberg. The ship shook, but most of the passengers were sleeping and were not disturbed.

The Chief Stoker was inspecting the boiler room after the collision, when he saw water pouring through a gash in the ship's hull. The tragedy of the *Titanic* was about to unfold.

From *Ideas and Issues Pre-Intermediate* by G. Sweeney (Chancerel). Past continuous and past simple.

2.2 Tense and time

Tense does not mean time. There often is a correspondence, but look at these:

*Sanchez **scores** the winning goal.*	present simple for past time	headline/caption
*And this guy **walks** over and **says** ...*	present simple for past time	popular narrative style
*Water **boils** at 100 degrees.*	present simple for all time	scientific fact
*Our coach **leaves** at 9 tomorrow.*	present simple for future time	timetable
*They **are meeting** us after the show.*	present continuous for future time	future arrangement
*I **was wondering** if I might ...*	past continuous for present time	informal request/query

2.3 Form and use (function) of tenses

The **form** of a tense, i.e. what grammatical words and morphemes (parts of words) it is made up of, is dealt with in this book as the case arises. We already know from chapter 1 that in *A new day **was** dawning*, *was* is the verb *be* acting as an auxiliary verb, which contains the tense, here PAST, and *dawning* is an *-ing* participle. We now know that the *tense* formed in this way is the **past continuous**.

By **use** of a tense we mean what it is used for in communication. The uses in our general tables are restricted for simplicity; more uses are shown later.

2.4 The continuous aspect

The terms *simple* and *continuous* (and later, *perfect*) are known as **aspects**. In some grammar books the term *progressive* is used instead of *continuous*, but most teachers seem to prefer the latter. The full title of the tense in *She is taking a course now* is actually PRESENT TENSE, CONTINUOUS ASPECT, but most teachers say PRESENT CONTINUOUS TENSE as this is less cumbersome.

Note: *simple* simply means *not continuous*. It is helpful in ELT when contrasting both aspects, otherwise it is technically redundant.

2.4.1 Form of the continuous aspect

	The **tense** is contained in the aux. verb.	
PRESENT	*is*	

	Aux. *be* + *-ing* participle make up the **continuous** aspect.	
PRESENT CONTINUOUS	*is*	*working*

PAST CONTINUOUS	*was*	*working*
FUTURE CONTINUOUS	*will be*	

Remember that grammar has little respect for semantics (meaning), being more concerned with form and syntax (the order of words). *I **walked** for ten hours* has quite a continuous meaning but the tense of the verb is past <u>simple</u> because of its form. *I **was walking*** is the past <u>continuous</u> tense just because it has the verb *be* and the *-ing* participle.

Re the form of the future continuous, it may be helpful to think of *will be* as one word for the time being.

2.4.2 Use of the continuous aspect

The use of the continuous aspect is difficult to explain briefly, but it mostly conveys *incompleteness*, while the simple focuses on the *wholeness* of events. Of course, at lower levels the word *continuous* itself will suffice, as long as contextual and visual helps (see 2.9) are offered to illustrate specific uses such as, in the past tense, to show that the event is concurrent with or interrupted by another.

2.5 Uses of the present continuous

Task 2.1   Three of the rows below are mismatched. Match them correctly.

EXAMPLE	USE
1. *She's going to the cinema. Look.*	a) temporary state/situation (present simple would convey permanence)
2. *I'm building a boat in my spare time.*	b) happening at time of speaking
3. *She's going to the cinema tonight.*	c) future arrangement
4. *He's always mowing his lawn.*	d) with *always*, an air of irritation may be implied
5. *We're living in Las Vegas.*	e) ongoing activity

2.6 Uses of the past continuous

Task 2.2   Three of the rows below are mismatched. Match them correctly.

EXAMPLE	USE (IN PAST TIME)
1. *At eight fifteen? I was watching the soap on the telly. I'm innocent.*	a) in progress over a specified length of time (not completed)
2. *The sun was setting as I left the ranch.*	b) a simultaneous or 'background' event for the main one
3. *We were discussing humanism all morning.*	c) with this verb more a state than an action; corresponds to AmE *had on*
4. *I was stirring the mixture and it just solidified.*	d) a durative action interrupted by an instant one
5. *She was wearing a rugby jersey.*	e) in progress before and usually continuing after a specified point in time

---

4   Work with a partner. Follow these instructions.

    a)   Write down three true sentences and one false sentence to describe what you were doing yesterday at each of these times: *7.30 am; 1.00 pm; 6.00 pm; 11.00 pm.*

    b)   Ask each other questions beginning *What were you doing at ... ?*

    c)   Guess which of your partner's answers is false.

From *Inside Out Pre-intermediate* by S. Kay et al (Macmillan). Past continuous 'call my bluff'.

2.7 Uses of the future continuous

Task 2.3 Three of the rows below are mismatched. Match them correctly.

EXAMPLE	USE (IN FUTURE TIME)
1. *At eight fifteen? I'll be watching the soap on the telly. Can you leave it till later?*	a) in progress before and usually continuing after a specified point in time
2. *I'll be passing your house on the way home; do you want a lift?*	b) stating matter of course rather than a plan or promise; keeping polite distance
3. *Don't go there now – they'll be doing their homework.*	c) stating matter of course rather than a plan or promise; showing business 'distance'
4. *Will you be teaching the lower group?*	d) 'supposition', or 'predicting the present'
5. *We'll be contacting you/You will be hearing from us in due course.*	e) enquiring about matter of course, showing no request intended

2.8 Review present, past and future tenses

Now read the abridged version of part 1 of *Tense Situations*, and this time pay attention to all the words in bold type.

TENSE SITUATIONS – PART I ABRIDGED

She is teaching.

Sue **takes (PRESENT SIMPLE)** photos of famous people.
At the moment she **is taking (PRESENT CONTINUOUS)** a course in ELT.

In 2003 her tripod **broke (PAST SIMPLE)**.
She **was taking (PAST CONTINUOUS)** a photo of the Sultan.

Her colleagues say she **will sail (FUTURE SIMPLE)** through her test.
She **will be presenting (FUTURE CONTINUOUS)** a lesson on the past tense.

Task 2.4 Fill in the tenses in the right hand column below, following the example.

0. *It went okay.*	*past simple*
1. *She'll be coming round the mountain.*	
2. *I'm looking forward to that.*	
3. *I left my heart in San Francisco.*	
4. *We export our problems.*	
5. *She was thinking of going next week.*	
6. *You'll never walk a loan.*	

2.9 The time line

You may wish to use what is usually called a *time line* to illustrate problem tenses:

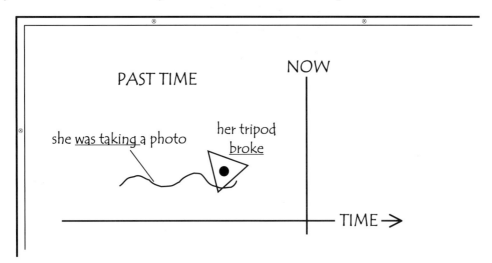

Figure 1. Time line for past continuous and past simple.

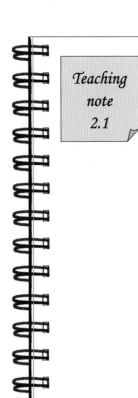

Teaching note 2.1

Research shows that spoken explanation (auditory intake) alone can be insufficient for learning. Time lines provide visual associations and certainly break the monotony of the one medium. The time line above shows how a single-action past activity (past simple) interrupts an ongoing one (past continuous). It may stop it completely, in which case the drawing would need just a little adjusting (the triangle would be a box blocking the end of the wavy line). In my diagrams I use a large dot inside a box (or triangle) to indicate the 'completeness' of the simple aspect time reference.

Please try to keep the blackboard neat for these visual helps. Write the word NOW, not PRESENT on the perpendicular line (present time does not always equal present tense!). Try to use capital letters for tense titles and other headings and lowercase letters for example sentences. It is not usually necessary, however, to include tense titles in time lines – the objective is to help the student to put the concept with the phrase/sentence, not with the tense title. In fact this is probably the essence of your job.

Try to give examples that are relevant or salient in some way – include topical events, students' names, your name, etc. And do remember the full stop at the end of a sentence (but not at the end of a phrase).

Remember, like most grammar aids, the time line is mostly for use as a remedial help, i.e. when a student is experiencing some difficulty with tense usage. If there is no difficulty, move on. Don't bore the students with your fascinating knowledge!

Finally, modern English language teaching prioritises communication. Grammar rules are utilised only as a help when required. The advice above – move on if there is no difficulty – would apply also to your use of the coursebook, should you be using one. Grammar awareness exercises which obviously bore or frustrate your students can be skipped.

Task 2.5 Draw a time line illustrating:
While I was watching TV the burglar stole my lesson plans.

3 Verb tenses 2:
Present perfect
Past perfect
Future perfect

3.1 Present perfect tense

The two sentences in part 2 of our story below exemplify the PRESENT TENSE, PERFECT ASPECT, or as we telescope it, the PRESENT PERFECT TENSE (with further SIMPLE and CONTINUOUS aspects):

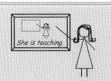

TENSE SITUATIONS – PART II

So far Sue **has written** (PRESENT PERFECT SIMPLE) two essays and four lesson plans.
She **has been working** (PRESENT PERFECT CONTINUOUS) hard for the last few weeks, studying, preparing lessons, surfing the job market.

Please note in the story that although the *writing* and most if not all of the *working* occurred in the *past time* the tense is called *present* perfect. In case you have difficulty with this remember:

    1. The auxiliary verb *have* is in the *present* tense;
    2. The action has a *present* relevance or consequence;
    3. The action occurs in a time zone up to the present.

The grammatical term *perfect* has little if any explanatory value for ELT.

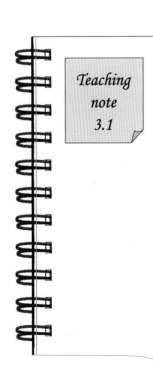

Teaching note 3.1

The present perfect tense in English, unlike many other related languages, does not allow mention of a past time (except with *since*), so concerned is it with the present. *Yesterday we have decided ...* is ungrammatical (as indicated by the prefixed asterisk). Even *This morning we have decided ...* is ungrammatical when the morning is over.

In contrast, the past tense must be accompanied somewhere in the discourse by a reference to past time. This is a simple but important difference often overlooked in teaching. WHEN A PAST TIME IS MENTIONED THE PAST TENSE MUST BE USED.

When teaching the difference between the present perfect and the past simple don't push too hard; a little now and again is better than a long tiring session. With good input, interesting topics and communicative activities it will look after itself.

Incidentally, by 'rich/good input' is meant meaningful interaction (and reading/listening) with language containing a good proportion of the targeted language.

3.1.1 Form of the present perfect simple

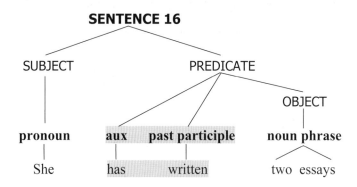

Please don't be distracted by the word *past* in *past participle*. The past participle can be used with any tense. The aux. verb here *(have/has)* is a primary auxiliary verb, not a modal.

> **past participle:** the third form of the verb, e.g.
> *broken* as in *break - broke - broken*, or
> *loved* as in *love - loved - loved*.
> (See chapter 12.)

3.1.2 Uses of the present perfect simple

In the example in our story, *she has written...*, we have only dealt with one use of the present perfect simple: **recent event with relevance to the present**. There is one more important use – **an experience or achievement** anytime in one's (present) life. An example of this would be *Sue has been to Peru*, or *Sue has photographed seven royal families*. You notice again we don't mention the past time as we are not concerned with it. What we are concerned with is *Sue*, in the present, through her experience. However, if we wish to shift the focus to the time of her experience we must use the past tense, e.g. *When did she visit Peru?*

---

1 The grammar in the following sentences is correct, but the sentences don't make sense. The endings have been mixed up. Rearrange the sentences so that they make sense.

   a) Have you ever ridden a snake?
   b) Have you ever been asked to the top of a mountain?
   c) Have you ever met a desert?
   d) Have you ever driven a television programme?
   e) Have you ever been to make a speech?
   f) Have you ever crossed a famous person?
   g) Have you ever appeared on a Ferrari?
   h) Have you ever caught a horse on the beach?

2 Work with a partner. How do you think your partner would answer each question?

   a) Yes, I have.
   b) No, never ... but I'd like to.
   c) No, never ... and I wouldn't like to.

From *Inside Out Intermediate* by S. Kay and V. Jones (Macmillan). Present perfect for life experience.

A time line can show the present perfect and past tense contrasted. The one below is slightly overloaded for economy of space – normally only two, sometimes three, examples are shown:

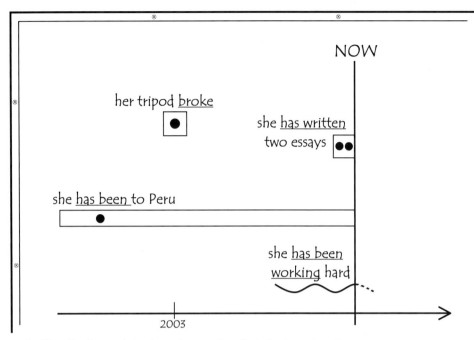

Figure 2. Time line for past simple and present perfect simple and continuous.

3.1.3 Form of the present perfect continuous

In the example *she has been working hard,* the first auxiliary, *has,* as usual, shows the tense. It is followed by the past participle of the second auxiliary *be,* then the main verb *work* in the -ing participle form

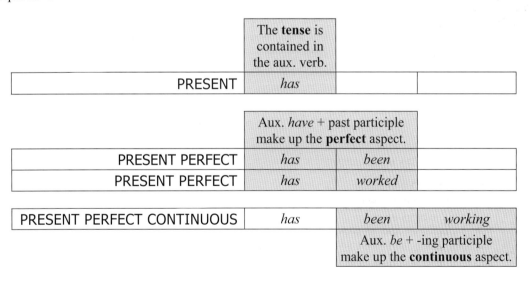

Compare and preview:

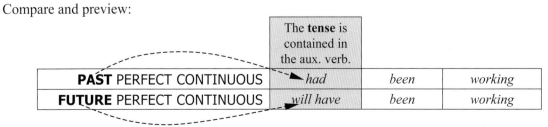

3.1.4 Uses of the present perfect continuous

The present perfect continuous refers to an activity (or state) continuous up to now. In the time line above, the wavy line is continued with dots to imply that the activity is not yet completed.

That use, however, refers mainly to when a time (e.g. *for the past three hours*) is highlighted. In another context the activity indeed may have stopped, e.g. the famous *Someone's been eating my porridge* (don't neglect storytime when teaching children) or *What have you been doing?* The activity itself and not its completion is the focus, hence the continuous aspect; the consequence is on the present, hence the present perfect. We shan't adjust the use 'continuous up to now' in our tense tables, however, in order to retain brevity.

Always have good examples ready when explaining. This one consisting of a doctor's questions would help in showing how the focus can be on either completion or continuity:

[1] *Have you taken the medicine?*
[2] *Have you been taking the medicine?*

See 4.3.2 for other considerations to be taken into account when explaining the present perfect simple and continuous.

From *Inside Out Resource Pack Upper Intermediate* (Macmillan). Present perfect continuous, guessing game (card holder is not allowed to say the underlined words in answer to yes/no questions). 18 cards in all.

Task 3.1

1. Draw a time line to show the difference between *since* and *for* in *We've been working here since January/for four months.*

2. Fill in the blanks:
   For and *since* are (a) p_____ of time.
   (b) _____ indicates duration; (c) _____ refers back to a starting point in time (there is one exception, where the perfect may be used instead of a starting time, e.g. *We have known her since we have lived here*).

   In informal use with certain verbs (d) _____ is often omitted, e.g. *We've been here five hours now.*

And now to update our list of tenses to include the present perfect, simple (s.) and continuous (c.):

TENSE	EXAMPLE	USE
present simple	*She takes photos.*	regular/habitual event; fact; job
present continuous	*She is taking a course.*	happening now (temporary)
past simple	*Her tripod broke.*	completed past event
past continuous	*She was taking a photo.*	'simultaneous' past event
future simple	*She will sail through her test.*	prediction of completed event
future continuous	*She will be presenting a lesson.*	prediction of 'simultaneous' event / happening as a matter of course.
present perfect s.	*She has written an essay.*	recent event / life experience
present perfect c.	*She has been working hard.*	continuous up to now

Teaching note 3.2

Although most British English textbooks stipulate only the present perfect with patterns such as *Have you done your homework yet? Have you ever been to Peru?* the past tense is also acceptable in AmE and some other varieties: *Did you do your homework yet? Did you ever go to Peru?*

In assessing English as an international language, then, one should not penalize the student for producing the past simple in lieu of the present perfect when there is no risk of ambiguity.

Task 3.2   Fill in the tenses in the right hand column below, following the example.

0. *It went okay.*	*past simple*
1. *I'll be with you now.*	
2. *I want it yesterday.*	
3. *He's seen the light.*	
4. *Are you joking?*	
5. *I wanted to know your name.*	
6. *You've been trying that all night.*	
7. *She'll be going up the wall.*	
8. *You weren't really listening.*	

3.2 Past perfect tense

TENSE SITUATIONS – PART III

Before enrolling on her course Sue **had considered** (PAST PERFECT SIMPLE) other career options but none of them really appealed to her.
She **had been browsing** (PAST PERFECT CONTINUOUS) the internet for some time before she clicked on an ELT banner.
She'd always had the feeling she'd like teaching, but hadn't known how to go about realizing her wish.

Part 3 of our story shows us the PAST PERFECT TENSE, with SIMPLE and CONTINUOUS aspects, or the PAST PERFECT SIMPLE and CONTINUOUS.

The terms *past perfect* and *pluperfect* are synonymous but the former is used in ELT.

When we are narrating a (past) event and we want to indicate that something else happened prior to the time of that main event (or series of events) we use the past perfect tense for this. A seeming exception is after *before,* e.g. *She grabbed the money before I had finished counting it* (i.e. when I hadn't finished counting it).

The past perfect can be seen as the past of the past, or the past of the present perfect.

The use of the past perfect continuous reflects that of the present perfect continuous (see 3.1.4 plus the time line below): the action can continue right up to the main past event or finish shortly before it.

By the way, on a matter of punctuation did you notice in *she'd always had the feeling she'd like teaching* above, that the contraction *she'd* can have two different expansions – *she had* and *she would*? Something similar also occurs with *she's,* etc. Contracted forms (short forms) are acceptable even in much formal written English now, and of course are taught from day one (*I'm a teacher, she's a nurse,* etc.).

The time line below uses arrows to indicate back reference from the past to the past perfect. The past perfect box has more than one dot to indicate repetition for this particular example. A stretched dot could be used for a durative event (e.g. *she had worked …*).

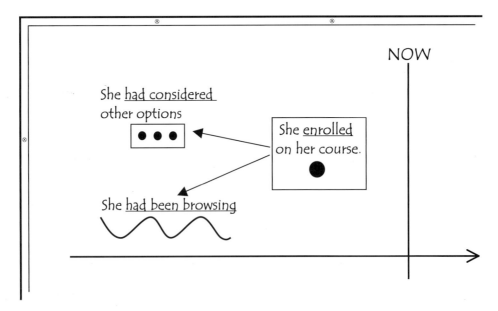

Figure 3. Time line for past perfect (simple and continuous).

Teaching note 3.3

Native speakers acquire the past perfect relatively late, so there's no need to 'push' it (except for exam classes).

One pleasant enough practice activity is to write on the board: *Everything was ready for the picnic.* Draw a car and elicit: *Dave had ...* (put petrol in the car). Draw a picnic basket and elicit *Ella had ...* made the sandwiches. With certain nationalities there may be claims of sexism to be enjoyed! Follow on with other items or friends/children. Then let pairs choose from *Everything was ready for the wedding/ bank robbery/product launch/fancy dress party*, etc, and write out some sentences. Compare. Don't forget to do one yourself. And do allow development of the story into the past simple; there's no need to insist on a battery of past perfect sentences.

Past perfect

1 Work in groups. Read the lateral thinking story below and discuss what you think happened.

In the middle of some grass lay a carrot, a scarf and some coal. No one had put them on the grass, but there was a perfectly good reason why they were there. Explain.

1 Match the beginnings of the sentences in A with the endings in B using *so* or *because*. Then write out the sentences with the correct form of the verbs in brackets.

Examples:
She spoke French well because she had lived in Paris as a child.
I had left my umbrella at home so I got really wet.

A
1 She (speak) French well
2 I (leave) my umbrella at home
3 My uncle (not want) to move
4 There (be) no food in the house
5 My grandparents (never fly) before
6 When I (get) home my father was angry
7 They (already sell) all the tickets
8 We (not have to) queue in the restaurant

B
a we (not get) into the concert.
b they (be) nervous when they got on the plane.
c I (not) phone him.
d I (forget) to go to the supermarket.
e my uncle (reserve) a table.
f she (live) in Paris as a child.
g he (live) in the same house for forty years.
h I (got) really wet.

From *New Cutting Edge Intermediate* by S. Cunningham & P. Moor. © Pearson Education Ltd 2005. Past perfect simple.

Task 3.3 Fill in the tenses in the right hand column below, following the example.

0. *It went okay.*	*past simple*
1. *I hadn't been abroad before that.*	
2. *He had a cold.*	
3. *Has he been bothering you?*	
4. *They've had the boat 3 years now.*	
5. *She'd been wondering about the price.*	

3.3 Future perfect tense

TENSE SITUATIONS – PART IV (FINAL)

Sue is doing well on her course. By the end of next week
she **will have mastered** (FUTURE PERFECT SIMPLE) how to teach relative
clauses, the conditionals and other points without 'teaching grammar'.
Her course leader, Alan, will also have reason for celebration soon: by the
end of this course he **will have been training** (FUTURE PERFECT
CONTINUOUS) at the same school for 25 years!

Part 4 of our story shows the FUTURE PERFECT TENSE, which completes the basic list of tenses.
We use the future perfect to look back on a recent event or life experience from a future point in time (compare with the present perfect). The future perfect may also be used to express the likelihood of the completion of an event (at a distance) before now, e.g. *They **will have arrived** by now.*

Now that you are at an advanced level you'll probably have been studying for quite a number of years. You'll feel fairly confident in being able to put your point across in most situations and won't have any problems talking to native speakers.

However, a native speaker with a strong regional accent will sometimes give you some trouble. You'll have been using cinema and television to give you practice in listening and no doubt you will have bought magazines and newspapers in

English to read in your spare time. You will possibly also have read a few novels or short stories. Maybe you'll have made English speaking penfriends or cyberpals and possibly you will have been invited to spend a holiday with them.

From *Inside Out Advanced* by C. Jones & T. Bastow (Macmillan). Future perfect.

Task 3.4 | Identify the future perfect verb phrases in the extract above.

Time now to see all the perfect tenses in our list. A highlighter or two would help if you are having difficulty recognising the tenses, for example highlight 'past perfect' and the aux. *had* in one colour; highlight 'continuous' and the aux. *be* plus the -ing participle in another colour).

TENSE	EXAMPLE	USE
present perfect simple	*She has written two essays.*	recent event / life experience
present perfect cont.	*She has been working hard.*	continuous up to now
past perfect simple	*She had considered other options before choosing ELT.*	completed event before main past reference
past perfect cont.	*She had been browsing the internet.*	continuous before main past reference
future perfect simple	*She will have mastered relatives by the end of next week.*	predicted to have happened by a future time
future perfect cont.	*Alan will have been training there for 25 years.*	continuous action up to a future time (duration stated)

4 Verb tenses 3:
Future markers
Review tenses
Stative and dynamic verbs

4.1 Four future markers

English doesn't have a future <u>tense</u> in the strict sense of inflecting the verb itself. We have met *will*, a modal auxiliary verb, and the present continuous for future arrangement (2.5), but there are four markers generally used to indicate future time shown below (for *shall* see 4.1.2). Note that with some speakers, especially AmE, *going to* is used instead of *will* in 3 and 5.

MARKER	EXAMPLE	USE
will (usually as *'ll* after pronouns)	} 1. *We'll play, we'll play, don't worry.*	promise, threat
	} 2. *I'll get it.* **Will** *I open it?*	offer
	} 3. *Rain **will** fall in the west.* *They'll need more time.*	prediction (fact)
	} 4. *No buses? I'll get a taxi, then.*	spontaneous decision
	} 5. **I think I'll** *go for a coffee.**	tentative decision
going to + verb (*be going* + infinitive)	} 6. *We're **going to** play our hearts out.*	plan (already decided)
	} 7. *Look out! It's **going to** fall!*	'obvious' future event
present continuous	} 8. *They're **playing** here on Saturday.* *We're **going** to the zoo tomorrow.*	arrangement ('diary' future), usually mentioning time
present simple	} 9. *Our train **leaves** at nine tomorrow.*	timetable

*The preceding *I think* is instrumental here, hence the bold font. This phrase is often used as a 'feeler', often with a following remark, to gauge the reaction, invite company, etc.

Other uses of *will* include:

That'll be Susie: supposition.   *The car won't start:* refusal.   *Will you do me a favour?:* request. *He <u>will</u> smoke where he shouldn't:* obstinacy.   *I'll have the miso soup:* choosing/ordering. *The PM will talk to the press after the reception:* formal announcement of schedule.

4.1.1 Forms and uses of *going to*

I'm <u>going</u> <u>to play</u> consists of the present continuous of *go* followed by the infinitive *to play*. This indicates a future **plan** (we call this **the 'going to' future**).

   I'm <u>going</u> <u>to the zoo</u> consists of the present continuous form of *go* followed by the preposition phrase *to the zoo*. The present continuous may indicate present activity or future arrangement.

   *We're **going to go** to the zoo* is the present continuous of *go* followed by the infinitive *to go*. Because both verbs are the same we sometimes avoid this phrase, but it does have its uses, mainly emphasising the plan/intention/decision itself, for example [1] explaining altered plans, or [2] replying emphatically to the question *What are you going to do?*:

[1] *We were **going to go** to the cinema but we went for a stroll instead.*

[2] *I'm **going to go** to the police, that's what I'm going to do!*

On the matter of teaching, most teachers say there is no great difference between, e.g. *I'm going to the cinema tonight* and *I'm going to go to the cinema tonight*, and for lower levels this may be true.

The frequency of use of the *going to* form obliges ELT grammars to include it as a future tense.

And finally, *be going to* is sometimes classified as a (phrasal) modal auxiliary verb. See 13.3.

4.1.2 Uses of *shall*

The use of *shall* for the future is heard mainly in parts of Britain. Coursebooks exclude it, except in the functions of suggestions and offers. A synopsis of its uses is fashioned into the table below.

As a rule of thumb *shall* is only used in the 1st person for predictions, sometimes promises (and suggestions and offers), and has restricted applications in the other persons. *Will*, for those who make the distinction, conveys volition, a willingness (*I won't open it* = it is not my will to open it).

	EXAMPLE	USE
1st person	*We shall be back after the break.*	prediction (/promise)
	I shan't get much sleep tonight.	
	Shall we eat Sichuan tonight?	suggestion
	Shall I open it for you?	offer
2nd person	*You shall have it.*	emphatic promise/order/threat
3rd person	*He shall die!*	
all persons	*The management shall not be responsible for any loss or ...*	officialese

TARA: What about Friday? I'm out in the morning but I've got nothing in the afternoon.

JENNY: Let me see … I've got plans but I can cancel … and I'm visiting another client in the morning so I could come straight to you in the afternoon. Is two o'clock OK?

FRANK: Hello, Ms Mueller. How are you?

SOPHIE: Fine, thank you … but … uh … I'm afraid my flight has been delayed. I'm sorry, but I'm not going to make it to Seoul in time for our appointment.

FRANK: Oh, dear. How long is the delay?

SOPHIE: They say two hours, but most of the flights are delayed. I think it's going to be longer than that.

FRANK: Oh, that's a shame. Well, shall we reschedule our appointment for the same time tomorrow afternoon?

MARTIN: You said you could possibly make Tuesday 4th or Thursday 6th?

KEVIN: Hold on, I'll just check my diary again … er, well, things have changed slightly. I can't do Tuesday now, but Wednesday and Thursday are OK.

MARTIN: Ah. Right, let me have a look … yes, that's OK, we can meet on Thursday 6th then. I'll confirm that in an email to everyone. Thanks, Kevin.

Tapescript extracts from *Business Goals 2* by G. Knight et al (CUP). Futures in arranging appointments and meetings.

Task 4.1 | Identify the future forms in the extract above and state their uses.

4.2 Review all tenses

Now we shall read the condensed version of our story, with the past perfect in a more comfortable position, for revision purposes. Try to match a mental picture with each tense.

TENSE SITUATIONS – CONDENSED

Sue **takes (PRESENT SIMPLE)** photos of famous people.
At the moment she **is taking (PRESENT CONTINUOUS)** a course in ELT.

On her first assignment her tripod **broke (PAST SIMPLE)**.
She **was taking (PAST CONTINUOUS)** a photo of the Sultan.

She **had considered (PAST PERFECT SIMPLE)** other career options before enrolling.
She **had been browsing (PAST PERFECT CONTINUOUS)** the net.

Her colleagues say she **will sail (FUTURE SIMPLE)** through her grammar test.
She **will be presenting (FUTURE CONTINUOUS)** a lesson on the past tense.

Sue **has written (PRESENT PERFECT SIMPLE)** two essays and four lesson plans.
She **has been working (PRESENT PERFECT CONT.)** hard since starting the course.

By the end of next week she **will have mastered (FUTURE PERFECT SIMPLE)** relative clauses, etc.
Soon Alan **will have been training (FUTURE PERFECT CONTINUOUS)** at the same school for 25 years.

Task 4.2   Fill in the tenses in the right hand column below, following the example.

0. *It went okay.*	*past simple*
1. *What will your Ma say?*	
2. *She'd waited as long as possible.*	
3. *Have you been clubbing in the caves?*	
4. *They'll have taken everything by then.*	
5. *I did everything I could.*	
6. *They'd been preparing to leave.*	
7. *I was looking to see if she was looking.*	
8. *Sally's gone back to her roots.*	
9. *How's it going?*	
10. *How long will they have been driving?*	

Task 4.3 Correctly reorder the information in the table below. Ideally, the list should be photocopied onto card and the sections cut out. Then the task may be performed individually or in pairs or small groups. This ensures more enjoyment, which usually ensures more learning (keep this in mind when your students are to do a matching activity). The first column should remain ordered as given.

TENSE	EXAMPLE	USE
1. present simple	a) *It'll be all right on the night.*	i) plan
2. present continuous	b) *We'd been trying to get it started.*	ii) predicted to have happened by a future time
3. past simple	c) *The plant had grown a foot in our absence.*	iii) continuous action up to a future time (duration stated)
4. past continuous	d) *They'll have been talking for ten hours come midnight.*	iv) prediction of 'simultaneous' event /happening as a matter of course
5. future simple	e) *I was just looking at it.*	v) prediction of completed event
6. future continuous	f) *You just never listen, do you?*	vi) continuous before main past reference
7. 'going to' future	g) *Neil stepped down.*	vii) regular/habitual event, fact
8. present perfect simple	h) *Bill will be seeing his secretary Monday.*	viii) recent event or life experience
9. present perfect cont.	i) *How long have you been telling that joke?*	ix) happening now (temporary)
10. past perfect simple	j) *That's torn it.*	x) completed event before main past reference
11. past perfect cont.	k) *She's standing her ground.*	xi) 'background' past event
12. future perfect simple	l) *They'll have destroyed half the rainforests by 2020.*	xii) continuous up to now
13. future perfect cont.	m) *You're not going to watch Star Wars again, are you?*	xiii) completed past event

Teaching note 4.1

Many teachers trained intensively in the communicative approach concentrate greatly on spoken skills, tending to forget that writing is communication also. It adds variety, can be a 'settler', allows the quieter ones to shine and consolidates what has been learned orally.

Short written tasks also provide material for further free practice and discussion. The postcard below shows three tenses for practice. Show it or similar ones (on board/OHP), pointing out the tenses and brainstorming more 'tourist' verbs like *see, visit, dance, eat, swim, buy, meet,* etc. Elicit the city/country and the sites mentioned, then ask students to write their own postcard with the same tenses and similar time adverbs. If a student is experiencing difficulty show them some pictures of famous places with sites marked (prepare these in advance). When finished, students read out and discuss, in groups if the class is large.

Tip: once you have checked students are ok (look at their work in progress) write one or two postcards yourself on the board/OHP while they are busy. Accept present continuous instead of 'going to' – there's not always a great difference.

Having a wonderful time here.

We <u>have seen</u> the place where the king's wife lost her head.

Yesterday we <u>went</u> up in the big wheel beside the river.

Tomorrow we're <u>going to take</u> a trip to the home of the famous playwright.

From an idea in *Top Class Activities* by P. Watcyn-Jones (ed.) (Penguin).

Try this one: *Having a wonderful time here. We have eaten tortilla, but it doesn't have egg or potato. Yesterday we saw some pyramids. Tomorrow we're going to listen to a mariachi band.*

Or this one: *Having a wonderful time here. We have travelled with dogs. Yesterday we visited the place where the generous man lives. Tomorrow we're going to sit in a hot place, then jump into a cold place. They say they invented the hot place.*

4.2.1 A table of tenses for students

The material in this book is not designed for students, but I am aware of the requests made by the grammatically minded for a compact list of tenses and I offer this for what it's worth. It is not suitable for a lesson; it is mainly a checklist for those inclined to learn in that way.

A TABLE OF ENGLISH VERB TENSES, WITH SOME EXAMPLES AND USES

TENSE	EXAMPLE	USE
present simple	*She **walks** to work.* *We **leave** for the airport at nine.*	regular event, job, fact timetable
present continuous	*She **is playing** well at the moment.* *We **are playing** tennis tomorrow.*	happening now (temporary) future arrangement
past simple	*Neil **stepped** onto the moon and said the immortal words.*	completed past event (a past time is mentioned)
past continuous	*I **was stepping** into the bath when the phone rang.*	'background' past event
future simple	*Rain **will fall** in the west.* *I'**ll wash** them later.*	prediction of completed event promise / instant decision
future continuous	*Karl **will be doing** his homework when you call.*	prediction of 'simultaneous' event / happening as a matter of course
'going to' future	*She's **going to burn** it again.*	plan / 'obvious' future
present perfect simple	*He **has eaten** the whole pizza.* *He **has written** twenty novels.*	recent event with present relevance (a past time is not mentioned) life experience
present perfect cont.	*I **have been wearing** glasses since my 21st birthday.*	continuous up to now
past perfect simple	*When we came home we saw that the cat **had eaten** the fish.*	completed event before main past reference
past perfect cont.	*She **had been looking** forward to meeting John but now this news turned desire to dread.*	continuous action before main past reference
future perfect simple	*They **will have destroyed** half the rainforests by 2020.*	predicted to have happened by a future time
future perfect cont.	*They **will have been talking** for ten hours by midnight.*	continuous action up to a future time (duration stated)

4.3 Stative and dynamic verbs

4.3.1 Stative verbs

When a verb has a **stative** sense it usually **cannot occur in a continuous tense** (e.g. **I am believing in God*). Below is a table of most of the verbs that have or can have a stative sense.

mental & emotional states	*believe, doubt, feel* (opine), *imagine, know, like, love, hate, prefer, realize, remember, see* (understand), *think* (opine), *want, wish*
senses	*appear, hear, look* (seem), *see, smell, sound, taste*
reactions etc.	*(dis)agree, deny, impress, mean, promise, satisy, surprise*
description, possession, etc	*be, belong, concern, consist, contain, depend, deserve, fit, include, involve, lack, matter, need, owe, own, possess, weigh* (have weight)

Verbs that relate to activity or change are called **dynamic verbs.**

The rule is flexible to a degree, e.g. a certain continuity or process/dynamism is carried by *Are you understanding me?* And the present perfect continuous is less restrictive, e.g. *I have been meaning/wanting to tell you this for ages.*

The examples below show that [1] the verb *like* is always stative, but *think* can be used [2b] statively or [2c] dynamically. The grammar in the remainder of [2a] and [2c] is also different.

        [1] **I am liking you.*
        [2a] **I am thinking you are nice.*
        [2b] *I think you are nice.*
        [2c] *I am thinking about it.*

Task 4.4   Explain how *We are being cold* may or may not be acceptable.

---

❷ How long have you known people? Write sentences.

▶ *I've known my English teacher since September*

1 I've known .... for ....

2 I've ....

3 I've ....

---

❸ How long have you had things? Write sentences.

▶ *I've had these shoes for six months*

1 I've had my .... since ....

2 ....

3 ....

❷ **Make questions beginning with *How long ...?***

▶ you / study / maths   *How long have you been studying maths?*

1   Jane / talk / on the phone ....

2   your brother / work / in Glasgow ....

3   Eric / drive / buses ....

4   that man / stand / outside ....

Reproduced by permission of Oxford University Press
From *The Good Grammar Book* by © Michael Swan and Catherine Walter 2001 (OUP). Present perfect continuous for 'continuous action up to now' (with dynamic verbs).

4.3.2 Dynamic verbs – durative (continuous act)

Verbs such as *live, work, rain, stay, talk, sleep, study, sing, teach* are **durative** because they give no indication of their duration/termination. This property becomes most noticeable when the difference between the present perfect simple and continuous is almost neutralised by the aspect of continuity within the verb itself. Observe:

[1] *We have lived here for 10 years.*
[2] *We have been living here for 10 years.*

Task 4.5	A student at upper intermediate level asks you to explain the difference in meaning, if any, between [1] and [2] above. How do you reply?

4.3.3 Dynamic verbs – punctual (single/repetitive act)

Verbs such as *jump, slam, throw, kick, nod, stab* depict momentary events. Used in the continuous aspect they indicate repetition, e.g. *Robbie was kicking the ball.* The simple form requires context to convey once-off or repetitive action, e.g. *Robbie kicked the ball to David; Robbie kicked the ball around.*

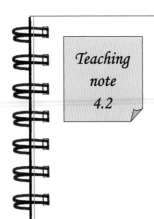

Teaching note 4.2

English, unlike other European languages, doesn't have an imperfect tense to convey duration, and some students may experience difficulty in their search for a corresponding form, experimenting with the past continuous etc. The verb *push,* for example, can be durative or punctual, so the duration of the pushing in *He pushed the trolley* is unclear. We have to resort to phrases such as *He gave it a push* to convey single act. Other languages may have neater ways of doing this.

When students are slow to produce a sentence be aware of the language processing going on in their minds. Give them time, if the delay is not embarrassing, and provide plenty of listening.

Task 4.6	A Spanish student at intermediate level writes:
	Also, in Spain I was working 2 years as a tour guide after finish my tourism studies. Later I ...
	Explain the two errors using grammatical terminology and suggesting a reason (based on guessing the structure of Spanish). For the second error offer *finishing* as the correct form and refer to 1.11 and task 1.6.

5 Nouns

In this chapter we will look at three categories of noun:

   1) **Countable/uncountable**   2) **Collective**   3) **Irregular**

5.1 Countable and uncountable nouns

5.1.1 Definition

What is the difference (grammatical) between *apple* and *serenity*? You can say *an apple/three apples* but you can't say **a serenity/three serenities*. We use the terms **countable** and **uncountable** for these two major classes of noun. As a broad definition, countable nouns can be counted (and *a/an* means *one*), and used in the singular or plural. Uncountable nouns cannot be counted and take only singular verbs.

5.1.2 Consequences

This countable/uncountable quality determines the accompanying quantifier *(many/much, a few/a little* – see next chapter) and article, and influences partitives such as *a bunch of, a bar of,* etc.

COUNTABLE	UNCOUNTABLE
cake(s)	*cake*
yoghurt(s)	*yoghurt*
sheep	*sand*
people	*wool*
phenomenon(-na)	- - - - - - - - - - - - -
child(ren)	*honesty*
month(s)	*physics*
suggestion(s)	*chess*

As the table shows, uncountable nouns may be divided into **mass nouns** (above the dotted line) and **abstract nouns** (below it). Some abstract nouns may be countable of course, e.g. *production*.

Task 5.1
1. Give two example phrases, one showing a countable context for *cake*, the other uncountable.
2. Which of the countable nouns in the above table is always plural?

5.1.3 Alternative countable and uncountable interpretations

a) **units vs. mass**
   some/four cakes, cabbages, lambs : some cake, cabbage, lamb
b) **measures, etc.**
   three teas/sugars/yoghurts means *three cups of tea, lumps of sugar, tubs of yoghurt,* etc.
c) **classifications**
   the wines of Province; a low-fat cheese, etc. : *wine, cheese*
d) **artistic/literary product vs. activity**
   some/four works of Goya : do some work
e) **situation(s) vs. state**
   got into difficulties (usually plural) : *had no difficulty (in) finishing*

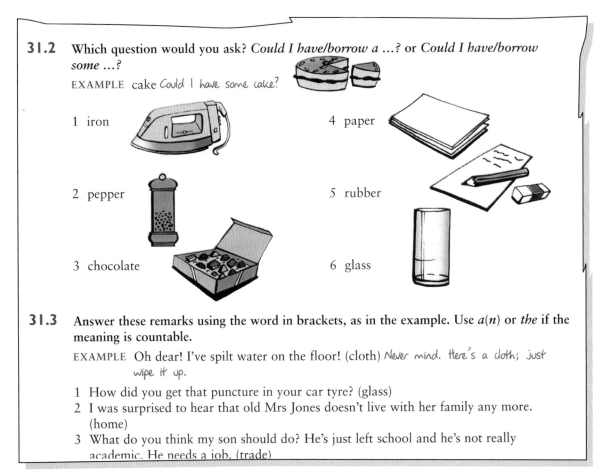

31.2 Which question would you ask? *Could I have/borrow a ...?* or *Could I have/borrow some ...?*

EXAMPLE cake *Could I have some cake?*

1 iron

2 pepper

3 chocolate

4 paper

5 rubber

6 glass

31.3 Answer these remarks using the word in brackets, as in the example. Use *a(n)* or *the* if the meaning is countable.

EXAMPLE Oh dear! I've spilt water on the floor! (cloth) *Never mind. Here's a cloth; just wipe it up.*

1 How did you get that puncture in your car tyre? (glass)

2 I was surprised to hear that old Mrs Jones doesn't live with her family any more. (home)

3 What do you think my son should do? He's just left school and he's not really academic. He needs a job. (trade)

From *English Vocabulary in Use, Upper Intermediate* by M. McCarthy & F. O'Dell (CUP). Countable and uncountable alternatives.

5.2 Collective nouns

Collective nouns refer to groups and so are also called **group nouns**. They can take a singular or plural verb, accordingly as the members of the group are seen as united or separate:

> The government **is** intact.
> The government **are** of different minds on the issue.

American formal English, however, prefers the singular verb.

Other collective nouns include *army, audience, family, flock, group, jury, staff, team, company.* Please note that **animal groups** such as *herd, pride, gaggle,* etc, do not automatically fall under this category in ELT, though the term 'collective noun/name' is sometimes used for them.

5.3 Irregular forms

Nouns which usually cause problems are

1) **Nouns always plural,** e.g. *clothes, police, cattle, goods, arms*

2) **Pair nouns,** e.g. *trousers, scissors, glasses (spectacles), scales (weighing).* Some speakers treat some of these as singular, e.g. *The scissors is over there ; Have you got a pliers?* etc. However, the standard usage is *are* and *a pair of* with these (*a pair of scales* is rare, though, and the AmE *a scale* may displace the plural).

3) **Uncountable nouns ending in 's'** e.g. *news, measles, linguistics, athletics, darts* (game).

4) **Nouns ending in 's' which are singular or plural** (with some the meaning may be different for singular and plural), e.g. *means, series, barracks, headquarters.*

5) **Other nouns which are singular or plural,** e.g. *sheep, deer, aircraft.*

6) **Uncountable or plural,** e.g. *travel(s)* (plural usually refers to a person's time/experience travelling, usually for pleasure), *politics* (plural usually refers to political beliefs, operations).

7) **-*f* to -*ves***, e.g. *knife-knives, shelf-shelves,* but *roof-roofs,*and *hoof-hoofs/hooves,* etc.

6 Quantifiers

6.1 Definition

Quantifiers come under the heading of **determiners**. Determiners are words in the noun phrase that can come before an adjective (and noun). See 7.2, 8.1 and 21.1.

NOUN PHRASE

DET.   adjective   noun
many   *plastic*   *bottles*

Quantifiers, or quantitative/quantitive adjectives, are a closed set of words comprising *all, both, half, much, many, some, any, another, enough, either, more, a lot, few*, etc, and the numerals.

These words can also operate as pronouns. See 7.10.

Please have your ESOL dictionary to hand for help and examples in explaining the difference between *each* and *every, all* and *everything* etc, (*everything* is a pronoun – see 7.6).

6.2 *How many?* and *How much?*

+ countable noun	+ uncountable noun
~~How *much* knives?~~ How *many* knives?	How *much* cheese? ~~How *many* cheese?~~
~~A *little* dogs.~~ A *few* dogs.	A *little* sand. ~~A *few* sand.~~
a lot of/ lots of dogs	*a lot of/ lots of sand*

ELT coursebooks usually teach *How many...?* and *How much...?* accompanied by some corresponding countable and uncountable nouns at elementary level:

How many tomatoes are there in the bowl? How much milk is there in the fridge?

6.3 *Many* and *much* (and *lots of /a lot of*)

In the affirmative, *many*, and especially *much*, tend to be formal (notice the incongruity of *There was much trouble at that gig, man*). In informal English *lots of/a lot of* is preferred, and it's advisable to teach these early on because they can be used with both count and uncount nouns:

There are lots of/a lot of pennies falling out there.
There's lots of/a lot of rain falling out there.

There's lots of + plural, e.g. *There's lots of pennies,* is generally acceptable in informal spoken English. Note also that *Here's/There's the forms; Where's my jeans?* etc, are similarly acceptable.

6.4 *A few* and *a little* ∼ *few* and *little*

A few (strawberries) and *a little* (cream) would also be introduced in coursebooks with count and uncount nouns:

A few beers, a little music.

Not until intermediate level, however, would *few* (social workers) and *little* (funding) be on the syllabus, as the connotation of scarcity here has to be understood despite the almost identical form with *a few* and *a little*. Students should check these words in their bilingual dictionaries.

Few and *little* are often the formal versions of *not many* and *not much*. We may write *There are few students in the library* but we would likely say *There aren't many students in the library*.

Task 6.1

> *Fewer* and *less* are comparative forms of *few* and *little*, respectively. Do the same rules of choice apply to these comparative forms (i.e. must *fewer* always be used with countable nouns and *less* always be used with uncountable nouns)?

6.5 Partitives

Most quantifiers (and quantities, etc.) can be followed by the preposition *of* to refer to a quantity of a set. With definite referents this *of* is obligatory, with the exception of *all*, *both* and *half*:

definite: *most of the banks, few of my friends* ; *all (of) the banks, both/half (of) my friends*
indefinite: *most banks, few friends* ;   *all banks*

Under-use *(*most the inhabitants)* and over-use *(I don't know how much money, but *there was a lot of.)* are typical errors.

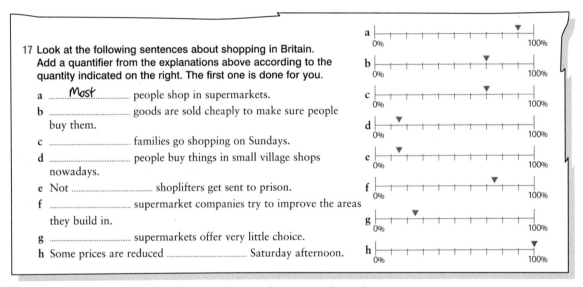

17 Look at the following sentences about shopping in Britain. Add a quantifier from the explanations above according to the quantity indicated on the right. The first one is done for you.

a ......*Most*...... people shop in supermarkets.

b .... goods are sold cheaply to make sure people buy them.

c .... families go shopping on Sundays.

d .... people buy things in small village shops nowadays.

e Not .... shoplifters get sent to prison.

f .... supermarket companies try to improve the areas they build in.

g .... supermarkets offer very little choice.

h Some prices are reduced .... Saturday afternoon.

From *Just Right Intermediate* by J. Harmer (Marshall Cavendish). Quantifiers.

Complete the sentences with (a) few, (a) little, the few, the little, what few or what little, giving alternatives where possible. (A & B)

1 Thomas was named sportsman of the year, and .... would disagree with that decision.

2 .... remains of the old castle walls except the Black Gate.

3 She called her .... remaining relatives together and told them she was leaving.

4 Simpson is among .... foreign journalists allowed into the country.

5 .... evidence we have so far suggests that the new treatment will be important in the fight against AIDS.

6 'Has my explanation helped?' '........................, yes.'

7 .... belongings she had were packed into a small suitcase.

8 .... will forget the emotional scenes as Wilson gave his farewell performance in front of a huge audience.

9 The announcement will come as .... surprise.

10 Tony hasn't been looking well recently, and I'm .... worried about him.

11 'Have there been many applications for the job?' 'Yes, quite ....'

From *Advanced Grammar in Use* by M. Hewings (CUP). Quantifiers.

6.6 *Some* and *any* with plural and uncountable nouns

To explain the uses of *some* and *any* at elementary level we can make do with the rule which says that **some is used in affirmative statements, and *any* is used in questions and negatives:**

> Tom's got **some** aardvarks.   *Have you got **any** tickets?*
> *We haven't got **any** sugar.*

There are some difficulties, however. Notice the use of *any* in the following affirmative sentence:

> *There's rarely **any** trouble.*

This is explained by pointing out that *rarely* (like *hardly, seldom,* etc.) is a **negative adverb.**

For exceptions such as *Have you got **some** money?* many teachers point out that a positive answer is expected. This suffices at lower levels, but for further analysis the terms **assertive** and **non-assertive** come into play (though their value in the classroom may be low).

Have you got some money? is 'assertive', because the implication is 'I think/assert you have or should have or will need a moderate amount of money.' *Have you got any money?* is 'non-assertive' and implies that there is only a possibility that you have money (and I may want some of it).

Would you like some banoffi pie? is a more 'assertive' offer than *Would you like any banoffi pie?* which more readily includes the choice of no banoffi pie.

6.7 Stressed *some* and *any*

Used with countable nouns *some* and *any* are usually stressed:

> *You'll make <u>some</u> woman a marvellous wife.   <u>Any</u> dream will do.*

Here the term **restricted** (type/quantity) for *some* and **unrestricted** for *any* are put into service. This has to be put into easier language for most classes, however, and clear examples may be the only way to ensure learning. The related indefinite pronouns (see 7.6a) provide similar examples:

> *<u>Something</u>'s gotta give.   <u>Anything</u> can go wrong.*

Some party! Some car! can be either complimentary or mocking as the intonation indicates.

Often occurring after a preposition *some* can convey a lack of interest:

> *He was talking about some car (or other) he was thinking of buying.*

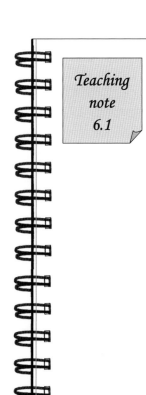

Teaching note 6.1

The person you most like to talk about is you. This fact is exploited in many learning activities such as information gap pairwork, discussion groups, guessing games, etc.

Another popular personalising activity involves getting students to imagine they are taking a journey and to observe their surroundings. This DREAM JOURNEY activity then concludes with a reporting and comparison in small groups of what they 'saw'. The teacher may play slow, soft background music and ask the students to imagine they are walking somewhere nice. "You see some trees" will prompt a later practice of quantifiers, as will "In the dining room there's a table with food on it."

Other valuable practice with descriptive language is gotten by suggesting but not stating colours, size, sounds (birdsong, musical instrument), smells (countryside, cooking), touch (climb over a wall, walk on the lawn/carpet).

The interactive part may consist of student A/B being 'analysed', their visualizations being interpreted, but this can be dangerous with sensitve students. You can instead ask groups to detect who is more visual, more tactile (some remember how the wall, carpet felt), more into food (some tables will be loaded with aromatic dishes, others just neatly laid for tea!) etc.

7 Pronouns

A pronoun 'stands for' a noun/phrase. Sometimes it can stand for a clause or sentence.

There are several **types of pronoun:**

1. **personal pronouns**	*I, you, he, she, it, we, they*
2. **possessive determiner pronouns (possessive adjectives)**	*my, your, his, her, its, our, their*
3. **possessive independent pronouns**	*mine, yours, his, hers, ours, theirs*
4. **demonstrative pronouns**	*this, that, these, those*
5. **reflexive pronouns**	*myself, yourself, herself, themselves*, etc.
6. **indefinite pronouns** **a. compound**	*somebody, anyone, no one, anything*, etc.
b. generic *one/you*	e.g. *One/you never know(s) these things.*
7. ***one* as count noun substitute**	e.g. *The one(s) in the window, please.*
8. **reciprocal pronouns**	*each other, one another,* *each/one ... the other, one ... another*
9. **interrogative pronouns**	*who, whose, what, which*
10. **quantifier pronouns**	*many, few, all, some*, etc.
11. **gender-neutral pronoun**	*they*
12. **pro-forms**	*so, neither/nor, not, then, there*
13. **relative pronouns** (see chapter 16)	*that, who, which, whose*

7.1 Personal pronouns

	SUBJECT		OBJECT	
	singular	**plural**	**singular**	**plural**
1st person	*I*	*we*	*me*	*us*
2nd person	*you*	*you*	*you*	*you*
3rd person	*he/she/it*	*they*	*him/her/it*	*them*

We have dealt with personal pronouns in chapter 1. The table is reproduced above.

An observation to be made at this time concerns the accepted breaking of the rules of case: the object case is preferred after the verb *be*, even though *be* is not a transitive verb. *It is I/he/she* sounds affected, unless there is a following clause, e.g. *It is I who should apologise*:

"*Who's there?*" "*It's me/her/him.*" is preferred over "*It is I/he/she.*"

Colloquial *give us a hand* instead of *give me a hand* is quite popular and learners at higher levels should be aware of it. The regional *yous* or *ye* or *y'all* (or *you guys)* indicates a desire for a clearly plural second person pronoun, but so far none of these has universal acceptance.

Task 7.1 A student asks which is correct: *between you and I* or *between you and me*. What do you say?

Task 7.2 | *It's getting late* is one example of *it* used as a 'dummy' subject, in this case for *time*. Can you think of at least one more referent for which *it* is used as a dummy subject?

7.2 Possessive determiner pronouns (possessive adjectives)

	singular	plural
1st person	*my*	*our*
2nd person	*your*	*your*
3rd person	*his/her/its*	*their*

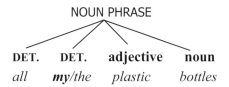

The title *possessive adjective* is actually more often used than *possessive determiner pronoun* but the latter is a more accurate description. Admittedly, in *his car*, the word *his* goes before the noun *car* and to that extent behaves as an adjective, but in **the his car* (compare *the old car*) it shows itself not to be an adjective; it certainly doesn't describe the car itself. *His* also stands for (pro) the noun *John's*, so also performs as a pronoun. Besides, most people would agree that these words 'look like' pronouns so the justification for calling them such is strong.

See 6.1 and 8.1 for more on determiners.

Note: although the term determiner is useful for grammatical analysis it is rarely if ever required in TESOL lessons.

7.2.1 *Its* or *it's*

Be careful with the spelling of *its*. The apostrophe indicates the shortened form of *it is/has*, not possessive:

> **It's** the dog that bit **its** tail.

For more on possessives see chapter 25.

7.2.2 Pronoun or definite article + parts of the body

> *A pigeon landed on **my** head.   That bloody pigeon got me on **the** head.*

Note how we can use either the possessive determiner pronoun or the definite article before a part of the body. With the definite article, however, usage is restricted to a preposition phrase following an object pronoun *(me)*, the context usually being an injury, touch, etc. (these restrictions need not apply in medical/scientific reports).

7.2.3 Possessive determiner pronoun + -ing form

> [1] *I didn't like **them/their** winning the cup.*
> [2] (?**Them**)/**Their** winning the cup proved that the championship was ...*

The use of a possessive determiner pronoun before a gerund lends formality. There is a free choice of this or object pronoun in [1] but the choice of object pronoun in [2] is not fully acceptable, certainly beyond the spoken level.

In a small number of grammars this possessive + gerund is called the *gerundive*.

Of course, there is a semantic distinction between, e.g., *I didn't like **them** singing* and *I didn't like **their** singing,* the former referring to the fact and the latter to the quality, so the choice is not always simply a matter of register*.

---

*Register is similar in meaning to formality or style. Register reflects the relationship between speaker and listener (or writer and reader).

7.3 Possessive independent pronouns

	singular	plural
1st person	*mine*	*ours*
2nd person	*yours*	*yours*
3rd person	*his/hers*	*theirs*

Students may require some time to acquire *a friend of mine*, etc, usually going through some normal error stages in the process. Just use gentle correction and TLC for painless progress.

We don't usually say *a bike/bag of hers* (unstressed), etc, but we do say *a friend/daughter/ student/play of hers,* etc, showing that what is possessed is usually a (indefinite) person or creative work. *Any/no bag of <u>hers</u>* (stressed), etc, is acceptable however, having a particular emphatic use.

From *Essential Grammar in Use* by R. Murphy (CUP). Possessive pronouns.

7.4 Demonstrative pronouns

This, that, these and *those* are adjectives before a noun (see 8.2.1) and pronouns on their own. They can be seen as 'pointers', referring to [1] physical things, or [2] part of the discourse:

> [1] *Is **this** yours? One of **these** is worth a hundred of **those**.*
> [2] *But **this** is only half the problem. **That's** not what I meant.*

The *this* in [2] would refer to an issue/situation close to the speaker in space/time; the *that* to one more removed, completed, a news item, an utterance, etc.

Some learners may seek a third demonstrative (equivalent to *yonder,* or something similar) before they get used to the common two demonstratives of English.

Demonstrative pronouns are also used to introduce people, point them out in a photograph, identify them on the phone (*this* and *that* only), qualify them (e.g. *with friends like **that** ...*), etc.

Task 7.3 | A student asks you to explain the difference between *It's a shame* and *That's a shame*. What do you say? Hint: use the term *preparatory subject.*

7.5 Reflexive pronouns

	singular	plural
1st person	*myself*	*ourselves*
2nd person	*yourself*	*yourselves*
3rd person	*himself/herself/itself*	*themselves*

We use reflexive pronouns as below:

[1] *Mary hurt **herself**.*	when subject and object are the same person
[2] *The house **itself** wasn't too bad.*	after the noun for emphasis, focus
[3] *She'll have to do it (by) **herself**.*	to mean *unaccompanied*
[4] *There was only Don, Liz and **myself***	often preferred at the end of a list of people
[5] *The row between **myself** and ...*	often preferred after *as, like, except, between ...*
[6] *What about **yourself**?*	to convey conviviality

After a preposition with abstract/idiomatic meaning, as in [7], the reflexive is common, but after a preposition of place, as in [8], it would be largely unacceptable:

[7] *You'll have to get a grip on **yourself**. Don't be so hard on **yourself**.*

[8] *Have you got any money on **you**? Take this with **you**.*

With certain everyday actions where the object is understood, the reflexive pronoun is often deleted:

[9] *He washed (himself), shaved (himself) and dressed (himself).*

Look out for malformations such as *hisself, theirselves*, etc, but see 7.11 below for *'themself'*.

In IrE, besides [6] above which is most common, the reflexive may be used for (mock) respect:

[10] *Is **herself** [your wife / the boss] in?*

But obviously this is for advanced level students only, and those with an interest in literature or linguistics.

7.6 Indefinite pronouns

7.6a Compound indefinite pronouns

Someone/body/thing, anyone/body/thing, everyone/body/thing, no one, nobody/thing, etc.

See 6.6 and 6.7 for the meanings of *some* and *any*.

Compound indefinite pronouns are singular, but may take a plural, gender-neutral pronoun (personal, possessive or reflexive) (see 7.11):

Everyone *was invited to take a copy away with <u>them</u>.*

Someone *is holding <u>their</u> hat in front of <u>their</u> face.*

No one *can set <u>themselves</u> up as a GP without a licence.*

French has the same word, *personne,* for *anyone* and *no one,* so selection problems are predictable.

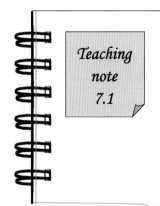

Teaching note 7.1

Don't underestimate the value of songs in language teaching. Children are the best language learners and it can't be coincidental that they enjoy storytime, role play and singing, excellent activities for listening and speaking.

Many songs include the words *someone, anyone,* etc. Lyrics and often the song itself can be got off the internet. Popular while-listening activities you can prepare are gap-filling, re-ordering lines, correcting wrong words, etc. Post-listening may involve discussion of the topic, writing another verse, role-play, etc. But don't forget the simple joy of singing. Children don't.

7.6b Generic *one/you*

One and *you* can mean 'people in general'. *One* is formal, and is often used in a moralizing or advisory tone. You use *you* for informal, especially oral instructions, directions, advice:

[1] ***One*** *must be sure of* ***oneself*** *in keeping up* ***one's*** *status, mustn't* ***one***?

[2] ***You*** *stir the mixture as* ***you*** *add the cornstarch.* ***You*** *turn left after the cinema.*

Note the reflexive and possessive forms of *one*. Also, as the example shows, the same pronoun - *one* - is kept throughout the sentence. The substitution of *you*, e.g. **One must keep up your status,* is unacceptable. However, in AmE *he* is acceptable as a substitute, e.g. ***One*** *must keep up his status.*

The pronoun *they* as in *You know what they say,* and *we* as in *If we really want peace why is there an arms race?* are also generic in that sense.

7.7 *One* as count noun substitute

The white/square ***one***.   *A black/round* ***one***.   *White* ***ones***.
The ***one*** *in the window.*   *A ***one*** *in the window.*   ***One(s)*** *with cheese.*

Popular teaching aids for this are coloured shapes, Lego or Cuisenaire Rods for 'total physical response' activities. Example: (pre-teach *the red/square one*, etc.) each of a pair of students has an identical set of mixed blocks/rods. Student A constructs a tower, unseen by student B (who has something else to do while waiting). Then student A gives instructions to student B to construct an identical tower. It is difficult! This activity sharpens language and awareness skills in an L1 class also.

7.8 Reciprocal pronouns

There is little if any difference between *each other* and *one another,* although certain collocations would indicate that *each other* is more personal, less formal, and often preferred for two:

[1] *They were made for* ***each other***.   *We love* ***each other***.

[2] *The members inevitably set themselves apart from* ***one another***.

With separated forms there is a similar preference:

[3] *Being like brother and sister* ***each/one*** *would always help* ***the other***.

[4] *Truckers are like that;* ***one*** *will always help* ***another***.

In any case be prepared to explain the difference (with good examples, of course) between, e.g.

[5] *They were praising themselves,* and

[6] *They were praising each other.*

---

4 **Explain the meaning of the phrases in blue from the reading texts.**

   a He made himself comfortable.
   b There was complete silence.
   c Everyone held their breath.
   d They flung their arms around each other.
   e The audience went crazy.

From *Just Right Intermediate* by Jeremy Harmer (Marshall Cavendish). Various phrases, some with pronouns (context: audience reaction). Phrases in blue underlined here for ease of recognition.

5 **Use the phrases from Activity 4 to answer the following questions. You may have to change the tense of the verb and some other words.**

   a What do you do when you swim underwater?
   b What do you do at the start of a long rail journey?
   c What might you hear in the middle of the Arctic or Antarctic?
   d What would you and your best friend do if you met after not seeing each other for a long time?
   e What would you do at the end of a concert by your favourite musician?

Task 7.4

Identify the pronouns in sentences a), c) and d) of activity 4 in the extract.

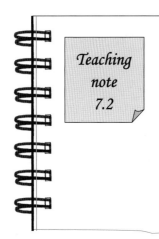

Teaching note 7.2

In the early days of TEFL a typical lesson would have as its objective an aspect of grammar (e.g. reflexive pronouns) or a language function (e.g. asking permission). This sadly led to an unvarying diet of that objective/targeted language throughout the whole lesson, stifling any move toward TOPIC. Normal language communication is driven by topic, not aspects of language. Check that you give prominence to a topic of interest in your class for an enjoyable, communicative lesson (apart from the <u>requested</u> grammar-centred ones). A little grammar in natural contexts over a time is better than force-feeding. See how the post-reading activity above from *Just Right Intermediate* raises awareness of three types of pronoun in a non-stressful way.

7.9 Interrogative pronouns

The question words *where, when, how, why* are adverbs so are not included here.

The difference between *what* and *which* may cause problems. *Which* is used when the choice is limited, but sometimes there is a free choice, depending on the perception of the limit (at the start of a noun phrase *what/which* is a determiner as in the second example below):

> **Which** do you want, the scone or the flapjack?
> In <u>**what/which**</u> <u>country</u> did the first World Cup take place?

Whose may present listening problems, being phonetically identical with *who's*.

7.10 Quantifier pronouns

All, both, each, either, enough, few, less, many, much, some, etc, besides acting as determiners (see 6.1) can stand on their own as pronouns.

Unless there's mention of an inanimate referent the countables usually have generic human reference:

> count: **All** *share your feelings* ; To **each** *his own* ; **Many** *are called,* **few** *are chosen.*
> uncount: **Much** *depends on it* ; **Little** *was known about* ...

All and *enough* are uncountable in *All I know/you need is* ... ; *All is lost* ; Enough *is enough,* etc.

7.11 Gender-neutral pronoun *(they)*

In older grammars, when a noun referred to an indefinite person its pronoun was *he:*

> Every teacher should have **his** lessons prepared.

Now, for PC reasons *he/she* is preferred, but mainly in the written medium, being cumbersone in speech, where *they* is becoming the norm:

> Every teacher should have **their** lessons prepared.

This is giving rise to a curious 'new' reflexive:

> How could anyone defend **themself** against ... *

Of course one may also use *he* or *she* alone for personal preference.

*Chicago Sun-Times 1991, in "Himself/herself or themselves" by S. Hayes in *Modern English Teacher* Jan 2004.

7.12 Pro-forms

A pronoun stands for a noun/-phrase. A pro-form stands for other constituents, but especially a phrase, a predicate or a clause. Most pro-froms are in fact adverbs but the term pro-form better describes their function.

Many pro-forms do not stand for an exact replication of the referent but substite for or add something on to a slightly altered form of it. So they are also called, especially in ELT, **substitute** or **additive forms**. The terms *pro-predicate* etc, below are my invention.

7.12.1 Pro-predicate

Agree pos + pos	Agree neg + neg	Disagree pos-to-neg	Disagree neg-to-pos
A: *I like grammar.* + B: ***So do I.*** + *(/I do too.)*	A: *I don't like grammar.* − B: ***Neither/Nor** do I.* − *(/I don't either.)*	A: *I like grammar.* + B: *Well, I don't.* −	A: *I don't like grammar.* − B: *Well, <u>I</u> do.* +

The most recurring pro-forms in ELT seem to be the adverbs *so* (substitute form) and *neither* (additive form), and indeed *nor* and *either,* all here roughly substituting for the predicate *(don't) like grammar.* Note the **inversion** (see 9.2.5) after *so, neither* and *nor*. The auxiliary *do* in *I do too* is in fact the pro-form there according to traditional grammarians, but such analysis is not necessary here.

    Nor is of low frequency in AmE. See 16.5 for *Neither ... nor ...* .

Jane: I've got a new boyfriend.

Tina: That's funny. So (1)..............................

Jane: Mine's very good-looking.

Tina: So (2)..............................

Jane: The problem is that he can't drive.

Tina: Neither (3)..............................

Jane: We went to the theatre last week.

Tina: So (4).............................. But he didn't like the play.

Jane: Nor (5).............................. He said he'd seen it before.

Tina: Then why did he go again?

From Instant Lessons 2 by D. Howard-Williams et al (Penguin). Pro-predicates (substitute and additives).

7.12.2 Pro-clause

The pro-clauses are ***so*** (substitute) for affirmative and ***not*** (additive) for negative, e.g.

hope, suppose	*why, if*	*why, suppose* (neg + neg)
A: *Is she going to give a speech?* B: *I hope/expect **so/not**.* B: *I suppose **so/not**.*	A: *She might give a speech.* B: *Why **so**?* B: *And why **not**?* B: *And if **so**?* B: *But if **not**?*	A: *She mightn't give a speech.* B: *Why **not**?* B: *I suppose **not**.*

We use the positive pro-clause *so* after *say* and *tell* (+ object), e.g. *I told you **so**.*
    We can use *not* after *say* only when this is preceded by an auxiliary, e.g. *I'd say **not**.*
    So can be used at the start of a sentence, e.g. ***So** I hear/believe.*
    Know or *be sure* do not occur with pro-forms. * *I know so/ I'm sure so.*

7.12.3 Pro-adverbial

The pro-adverbials are mainly *then, there* and *so*:

        [1] *They called at four, but we were out **then** (at four).*
        [2] *On 42nd Street? I'll be **there** (on 42nd Street).*
        [3] *Promptly they came, and **so** (promptly) did they act.*

8 Adjectives

8.1 Definition

Adjectives are words that modify nouns. Words that can come before modifiers of nouns are grouped as **determiners**, but teachers prefer the title *adjective* for most of these also, for example we call the first determiner below a quantitative adjective or quantifier (sometimes a quantifying determiner), and we call the second determiner a demonstrative adjective (sometimes a demonstrative determiner). Only a few quantifiers can go before a second determiner.

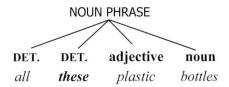

```
                    NOUN PHRASE

        DET.    DET.    adjective    noun
        all     these    plastic     bottles
```

8.2 Types of adjective - functional

TYPE OF SET	TYPE OF ADJ.	EXAMPLES/SET
CLOSED	demonstrative	(i) *this, that, these* and *those.*
	quantitative	(ii) *all, any, another, both, each, few/a few, many* ... (total approximately 20, not counting numerals or *of+* types).
OPEN	classifying	(iii) *electric, Korean, medical, oak, metal, pregnant* ..
	qualitative	(iv) *dark, efficient, friendly, fast, hard, funny, musical* ...

8.2.1 Demonstrative *them* instead of *those*

Them is equal to the demonstrative *those* (?*Leave them kids alone*) for many speakers, but this is not widely acceptable.

8.3 Types of adjective - grammatical

8.3.1 Attributive and predicative adjectives

These criteria pertain to the position of the adjective: [1] attributive is before the noun; [2] predicative is not before a noun and usually in the predicate. There may be some semantic change or restrictions:

[1] *the great famine : my elder sister : * the ablaze house*
[2] *?the famine was great : *my sister is elder : the house is ablaze*

8.3.2 -ing participial adjectives

-ing participial adjectives are derived from verbs and usually describe an affect:

amusing, interesting, demeaning, humiliating, tempting, tiring.

Adjectives ending in *-ing* which are derived from nouns, e.g *enterprising, neighbouring,* are not called -ing participials. (Note this hair-splitting is not for the ESOL classroom; however, a familiarity with the terminology is required for more relevant topics later, and for professional confidence.)

8.3.3 Past participial adjectives

Many past participles (sometimes called *-ed* or *-en* participles) can serve as adjectives:

amused, interested, fallen, embarrassed, forsaken, exhausted, pleased

Some words may look like past participles but they are adjectives only, having no corresponding verb, e.g. *downtrodden (*to downtread ...),* or being only partly related to a verb, e.g. *drunken.*

8.3.4 "There's nothing to do so I'm boring."

A common error is confusion between the -ing and past participial adjective. To explain the difference try pointing out that the -ing participle is causal, describes the effect of something (or even somebody) whereas the past participle describes the person's feeling/reaction. Your coursebook/grammar practice book will have suitable presentation/practice activities.

8.3.5 Noun as adjective

These nouns usually indicate material or function, e.g. *brick* wall, *music* room. Included here are gerunds (-ing forms as nouns), e.g. *swimming* pool, *racing* pigeon, etc.

8.3.6 Possessive adjectives

See 7.2.

8.4 Order of adjectives

When a number of qualitative and/or classifying adjectives occur before a noun, they usually follow a certain order. Below is a (rather overloaded) noun phrase with various sub-types of adjective.

Task 8.1

1. Sort out the noun phrase by matching each adjective with its type and putting these into an acceptable order.
2. Indicate which types would go under the macro types *QUALITATIVE* and *CLASSIFYING*.

	COLOUR	MATERIAL	NATIONALITY	SIZE	PURPOSE	QUALITY	
A	Victorian	old	ceramic	water	red	big	jug

Of course, the ordering rule can be broken somewhat for emphasis, etc.

8.5 Non-gradable adjectives

Adjectives at the end of a scale, such as *boiling* ↔ *freezing, huge* ↔ *tiny, brilliant* ↔ *awful, fascinating, incredible, terrifying, disastrous, brilliant,* etc, cannot be pre-modified with *very, fairly,* etc, but can be with *absolutely, really, quite,* etc. Those adverbs that can precede non-gradable adjectives are sometimes called *emphasizers* or *maximizers* (see 9.2.6c).

Classifying adjectives, e.g. *Korean, electric,* don't normally allow any modification. *Absolutely Korean, very Irish, really electric* are of course possible but the meaning is thereby changed to the quality rather than the classification.

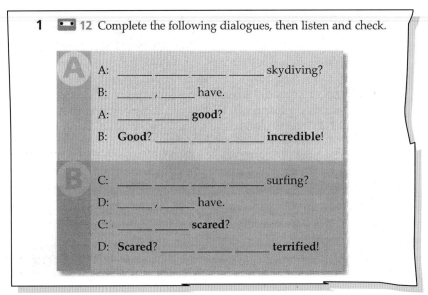

1 12 Complete the following dialogues, then listen and check.

A

A: _____ _____ _____ _____ skydiving?

B: _____ , _____ have.

A: _____ _____ **good?**

B: **Good?** _____ _____ _____ **incredible!**

B

C: _____ _____ _____ _____ surfing?

D: _____ , _____ have.

C: _____ _____ **scared?**

D: **Scared?** _____ _____ _____ **terrified!**

From *Inside Out Intermediate* by S. Kay & V. Jones (Macmillan Heinemann). Gradable and non-gradable adjectives.

9 Adverbs

9.1 Terminology, functions, formation

An **adverb** is a word giving us information about how, where, when or to what degree something is done, e.g. *do it **quickly**, go **out/home**, leave **today**, **completely** destroyed*.

An **adverbial** is an adverb <u>or</u> any group of words, not necessarily containing an adverb, which functions as an adverb, e.g. *as fast as possible, under the clock, after eight, unfortunately*. Please note that in this book *adverb = adverbial* where convenience allows.

Adverbs do a lot of work. An adverb can modify a verb, an adjective, another adverb, a whole sentence, even post-modify a noun (e.g. *kids **today***).

Some adverbs like *hard, fast,* are called irregular adverbs because they do not add the *-ly* on to the adjective form. Sometimes *quick, slow, tight,* etc, which are normally adjectives, can be adverbs, e.g. *Get rich **quick**; drive **slow*** (informal AmE); *shut it **tight***.

Task 9.1 | 1. A student writes *He ran cowardly from me.* Comment.

9.2   Types of adverb

In the table below some adverbs will occur in more than one category. This is a result of some categories not being mutually exclusive (e.g. 4 and 5), but also because some adverbs have a range of meanings.

TYPE OF ADVERB		EXAMPLES
1. manner		*slowly, quickly, peacefully, coolly, well, fast, hard*
2. time		*then, soon, yesterday, at two o'clock, all night, presently*
3. place and direction		*here, there, home, northward, below, abroad*
4. frequency		*always, often, sometimes, seldom, rarely, hardly ever, never*
5. broad negative		*hardly, barely, scarcely, seldom, rarely, never*
6. degree	**a. quantity**	*extensively, completely, partially, hardly ¦ much ¦ too, enough, so*
	b. intensifier	*very, extremely, really, so* (colloquial)
	downtoner	*fairly, sort of, quite*
	c. 'maximizer'	*absolutely, totally, quite, utterly, really, so* (coll.)
7. focusing		*only, just, (e)specially, mainly, also, too, neither, either*
8. 'completion aspect'		*still, yet, already*
9. dummy subject		*there*
10. discourse marker		Discourse markers are adverbials that modify the whole sentence, e.g. *suddenly, frankly.* See chapter 22.

9.2.1 Adverbs of manner

These have a great deal of flexibility regarding position:

> *(Hurriedly,)° she (hurriedly)° dressed (hurriedly)° for dinner (hurriedly)°.*
> *(?Loudly,)° the captain (loudly)° gave ~~loudly~~ his orders (loudly)° to the crew (loudly)°.*

Initial position is used more in writing, for emphasis or variety. It doesn't readily accommodate adverbs that focus somewhat on the perception of the activity.

9.2.2 & 9.2.3 Adverbs of time and place

These usually go in end position, but may be fronted for topicality or emphasis:

> *(Tomorrow)° they're coming here (tomorrow)°.*
> *(In Xian)° there are thousands of terracotta soldiers (in Xian)°.*

When together they can occur in any order, though place may tend to precede time, especially when the adverb of place is one of the closed set type (*here, there,* etc.):

> *I'll see you **there at nine**.*

Presently mainly means 'soon' in BrE but means 'now' in AmE.

9.2.4 Adverbs of (general) frequency

These go before the main verb, or after *be:*

> *She **rarely** <u>smiles</u>.   He <u>is</u> **seldom** right.*

They usually follow the (first) auxiliary verb:

> *She <u>has</u> **rarely** smiled.   I <u>should</u> **never** have told him.*

but they precede the semi-modal *have to,* and are flexible with *used to* (split infinitive permitting):

> *She **usually** <u>has to</u> share.   I (always)° <u>used</u> (always)° <u>to</u> (always)° go to Mass.*

These rules of position may be bent for emphasis (e.g. *she never <u>would</u> take the easy option*), and especially *sometimes, often* and *usually* can appear at the start or end of a sentence. In end position many frequency adverbs tend to be premodified with *very*. Other phrases usually go in end position:

> *She wears that ring <u>very</u> **seldom** now.   She wears it **all the time** now.*

Adverbs of definite frequency go in end position:

> *The post comes twice **daily**.*

> **Complete these sentences with ONE word in each space. Can you do this without looking at the examples above?**
>
> 1. A: Do you read a lot?
>   B: Yes, all the _____ . I usually read _____ least two or three books _____ week.
>
> 2. A: Do you go out a lot?
>   B: No, not that _____ – maybe once _____ two weeks.
>
> 3. A: Do you go to the cinema a lot?
>   B: No, _____ ever. I don't really like watching films.
>
> 4. A: Do you eat out a lot?
>   B: No, not _____ much – _____ once a month. I prefer to cook at home.
>
> 5. A: Do you watch TV a lot?
>   B: Yes, _____ the time. I _____ watch at _____ two or three hours a _____ .
>
> 6. A: Do you go to a lot of art exhibitions?

From *Innovations Pre-intermediate* by H. Deller & A. Walkley. © 2004 Reprinted with permission of Heinle, a division of Thomson Learning. Expressions of frequency.

9.2.5 Broad negative adverbs

These usually go in mid position:

> They can **hardly** throw us out.

They can also start a sentence, but this triggers **inversion**, i.e. instead of SUBJECT + (AUX VERB +) MAIN VERB the order is AUX VERB + SUBJECT + MAIN VERB:

> **Never** will I attempt that.   **Rarely** does she eat spinach without soy sauce now.

This applies to *hardly, no sooner, barely* and *scarcely* only as correlative coordinators (see 16.5). Inversion in fact involves the **operator**, which is the name given to the first auxiliary or *be*. *Seldom, rarely, hardly ever* and *never* are principally frequency adverbs.

9.2.6 Adverbs of degree

There is no agreement among grammarians on the subcategorisation of degree adverbs. I have posited three as in the table, according to collocation as much as semantics, e.g. *extensively renovated* forms good collocation but not ?*very renovated* or ?*absolutely renovated* (the collocation *sort of renovated* is fine of course, but the semantic property would be quality rather than quantity).

9.2.6a quantity

Adverbs of quantity or 'extent' modify verbs, adjectives or past participles (and some adverbs), but their collocations are not uniform, hence the boxes in the row in the table in 9.2. There may be some flexibility in position with a verb but not usually with an adjective or past participle:

> He (completely)° exonerated them (completely)°.
> **partially** deaf   **completely** exonerated by ...

Much, in questions and negatives, and *a lot* and *a little* mostly occur in end position:

> I don't go there **much**.   I like it **a lot/ a little**.

Much has a few common positive contexts, appearing pre-verb/participle. *Little* (formal register) shares the same spot:

> I **much** prefer ...   I **little** dreamt...   **much** maligned   **little** amused

Other quantity adverbs include *badly, dearly, noticeably, poorly, somewhat, well*.

The excessive *too*, the sufficient *enough*, and the comparative *so* mainly modify adjectives or adverbs:

MODIFYING AN ADJECTIVE	MODIFYING AN ADVERB
too hot (to handle)	**too** quickly (for us to keep up)
hot **enough** (to pour)	loudly **enough** (to be heard at the back)
so kind (a person) that ...	**so** much better, **so** generously that ...

9.2.6b intensifiers and downtoners

Very is the most common and versatile of the intensifiers. It can premodify (intensify) not only qualitative adjectives *(very cold)* and manner/time adverbs *(very quickly/soon),* but also some quantity adverbs *(very extensively)* and frequency adverbs *(very often).* When it premodifies *much* together these can take mid or end position:

> I (very much)° like the Sri Lankan teas (very much)°.

With an auxiliary verb especially and infinitive object a post-verb position is possible:

> I would (very much)° like (very much)° to visit Cuba (very much)°.

Very can also be a **restrictive adjective,** of course:

> The **very** thought of you ;   the **very** man I need.

In modern colloquial usage, **so** is acting for *very* to a much greater degree and with more syntactic freedom than it did in the past. For example, *I would **so** like to visit Cuba* sounds very 50's, whereas *I'm **so** not going to ask him out* is more of our time, albeit restricted to younger types.

Fairly, reasonably, pretty, rather, quite, etc, have nuances in certain contexts, suit a certain medium (spoken or written) and variety, e.g. *rather* (usually meaning 'more than usual/expected') is mainly restricted to BrE. The reader is advised to look these adverbs up in an ESOL dictionary or comprehensive reference grammar such as *Practical English Usage* (M. Swan) when planning classes with a focus on their usage.

9.2.6c 'maximizers' (emphasizers)

I have invented this title for adverbs that modify non-gradable adjectives (see 8.5):

>   ***absolutely*** *incredible,* ***totally*** *separate (totally and some others may have a restricted spread)*
>   ***utterly*** *trivial,* ***quite*** *amazing,* ***really*** *wonderful,* ***so*** *delicious, absurd, magnificent, etc.*

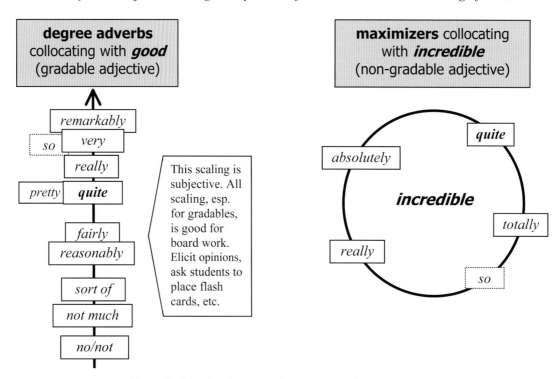

Figure 4. Adverbs with gradable and non-gradable adjectives.

As figure 4 above shows, *quite* has two meanings (in BrE), acting either as a low intensifier / downtoner with gradable adjectives (or adverbs) or as a maximizer with non-gradable adjectives (or adverbs). In AmE it is not a maximizer. *Really* has a somewhat similar spread:

>   *She speaks English **quite well** now.* (+ gradable adverb)
>   *It's **quite amazing** how little the town has changed.* (+ non-gradable adjective)

WHICH WORD?

also · as well · too

■ **Also** is more formal than **as well** and **too**, and it usually comes before the main verb or after *be*: *I went to New York last year, and I also spent some time in Washington.* In *BrE* it is not usually used at the end of a sentence. **Too** is much more common in spoken and informal English. It is usually used at the end of a sentence: *'I'm going home now.' 'I'll come too.'*. In *BrE* **as well** is used like **too**, but in *NAmE* it sounds formal or old-fashioned.

■ When you want to add a second negative point in a negative sentence, use **not...either**: *She hasn't phoned and she hasn't written either.* If you are adding a negative point to a positive one, you can use **not...as well/too**: *You can have a burger, but you can't have fries as well.*

Focusing adverbs with 'additive' function.

9.2.7 Focusing adverbs

These usually adopt the same position as frequency adverbs, but some have great flexibility:

>   *(Only)° I (only)° wanted (only)° to talk (only)° to Mary (only)°.*

Accurate placement of focusing adverbs is not a priority with most native speakers. They mainly prefer mid position and seem to rely mainly on stress to avoid any ambiguity.

9.2.8 'Completion aspect' adverbs

These are a type of time adverb. They usually merit their own slot in ELT coursebooks.

Still normally occurs in mid position, but can be flexible for emphasis:

> She **still** sucks her thumb. ~ She sucks her thumb **still**.

Yet occurs in end position, or after the negative adverb *not* in mid position, e.g.

> I haven't (yet)° seen a haggis (yet)°.

Already occurs in mid or end position, e.g.

> He's (already)° eaten it (already)°.

Yet is used with a negative, even when this is hidden, e.g.

> I have **yet** to see a haggis (almost synonymous with I have **still** to see a haggis)

But some formal or archaic non-negative uses of *yet* may yet be found.

In initial position and usually followed by a comma, *still, yet* and *already* are more akin to discourse marker, conjunction and time adverb respectively.

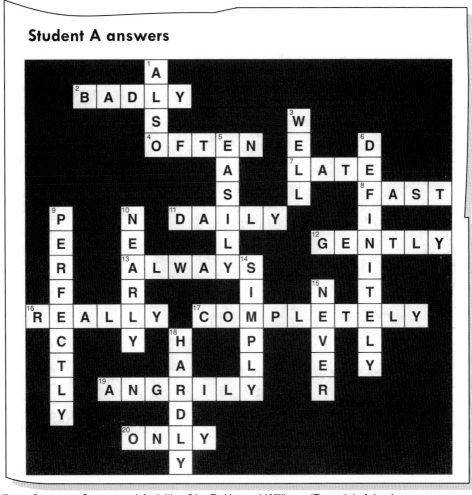

Student A answers

From *Grammar Games and Activities 2* by D. Howard-Williams (Penguin). Adverbs.
Students A write clues and pass them to students B who fill in their empty version, and vice versa.

Task 9.2 | Categorise the adverbs in the crossword above according to the types covered in this chapter. Some adverbs may be of more than one type.

9.2.9 Dummy subject *there* (existential *there*)

There is / there are are taught at elementary level. It's important to show the stressed place adverb *there (there's my school)* compared to the unstressed dummy subject *there (there's a school beside the mosque),* but don't introduce them both in the same lesson. See also 6.3.

10 Degrees of comparison

10.1 Comparison of adjectives

POSITIVE	COMPARATIVE	SUPERLATIVE
1. *fast* *happy*	*faster* *happier*	*(the) fastest* *(the) happiest*
2. *clever*	*cleverer/more clever*	*(the) cleverest/most clever*
3. *tragic* *intelligent*	*more tragic* *more intelligent*	*(the) most tragic* *(the) most intelligent*
4. *good* *bad* *much/many – little*	*better* *worse* *more – less*	*(the) best* *(the) worst* *(the) most – least*

e.g. *She is **faster** and **more intelligent** than the others. She is **the fastest** of all / Whoever is **(the) fastest** wins.*

Adjectives divide into 4 types for comparative and superlative formation as the above table shows:
1. Monosyllabic, or bisyllabic ending in *-y*: *-er*, *-est.*(with relevant spelling changes)
2. Bisyllabic usually with final 'soft' consonant (or other phonological properties which lend to ease of suffixation with *-er* and *-est*): free choice of *-er*, *-est* or *more, most*. Other examples are *common, gentle, narrow, pleasant, remote, stupid* (some mainly AmE and/or in the superlative).
3. Other bisyllabic, or polysyllabic: *more, most*.
4. Irregular.

10.2 Comparison of adverbs

POSITIVE	COMPARATIVE	SUPERLATIVE
1. *hard* *fast*	*harder* *faster*	*(the) hardest* *(the) fastest*
2. *quickly/quick* *slowly/slow*	*more quickly/quicker* *more slowly/slower*	*(the) most quickly/quickest* *(the) most slowly/slowest*
3. *intelligently* *often*	*more intelligently* *more often*	*(the) most intelligently* *(the) most often*
4. *well* *badly* *much – little*	*better* *worse* *more – less*	*(the) best* *(the) worst* *(the) most – least*

e.g. *She works **faster** and **more intelligently** than the others. She works **the fastest** of all / Whoever works **(the) fastest** wins.*

Adverbs divide into 4 types for comparative and superlative formation as the above table shows. All these are manner adverbs, except for the frequency adverb in 3, the quantity adverb(s) in 4, and the extra examples in 1. below:
1. Adverbs identical in form to adjectives: *-er*, *-est*. Other examples are *early, late, long, near, high*.
2. *-ly* adverbs with alternative adjectival form for informal and restricted uses:
choice of *more, most* + *-ly*, or *-er*, *-est*.
3. Polysyllabic including *-ly*, or bisyllabic without *-ly*: *more, most*.
4. Irregular.

10.3 Oddities

Task 10.1

Fill in the blanks:

The choice between *taller than I (am)* and *taller than me* is one of register*. The former is (a) _____ , sounding more affected when the verb *be* is optionally ellipted (left out).

Concerning *farther* and *further*, (b) _____ refers to distance only, whereas (c) _____ can refer to either distance or quantity.

As X as … and *not as X as* … are also used to compare and contrast. For the negative we can also use *not* (d) _____ *X as* … .

Lesser is a comparative of *little,* meaning smaller in size, status, etc. As an adjective it occurs only in attributive position (before the noun). It has restricted but popular collocations such as *to a lesser* (e) _____ / *of lesser importance* and with animals and birds. As an (f) _____ it most commonly occurs with *known.*

Besides marking the superlative form, *most* can act as an (g) _____ before adjectives, somewhat similar to *very,* e.g. *It was most unfortunate to lose like that.*

*Register is similar in meaning to formality or style. Register reflects the relationship between speaker and listener (or writer and reader).

Teaching note 10.1

'Information gap' is a popular principle of communicative language teaching. Try to ensure you include it in your discourse once the students understand the targeted language. For example "Who is taller, Pedro or Yoshi?" does not generate interest if the difference is obvious, i.e. there's no information gap. Choose students of similar height (and do have a measuring tape handy).

In time your stock-in-trade will include knowledge of the height of the Eiffel Tower and Statue of Liberty, the length of the Great Wall, etc. ... Okay, 320m, 93m including base and 2,250km.

2 The longest recorded flight for a chicken is thirteen minutes. ☐

8 The most popular pet in Great Britain is a rabbit. ☐

9 An ostrich's eye is bigger than its brain. ☐

15 The largest mammal is an African elephant. ☐

From *Grammar Games and Activities 2* by D. Howard-Williams (Penguin). Quiz (selection) including comparatives.

11 The passive

11.1 Definition and form

The passive is a particular sentence construction:

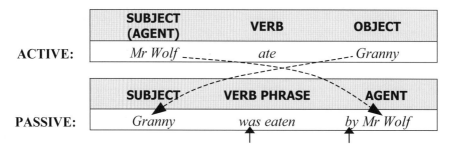

	SUBJECT (AGENT)	VERB	OBJECT
ACTIVE:	*Mr Wolf*	*ate*	*Granny*

	SUBJECT	VERB PHRASE	AGENT
PASSIVE:	*Granny*	*was eaten*	*by Mr Wolf*

To change a sentence from active to passive: a) move the object *(Granny)* to the position of grammatical subject (before the verb); b) insert the verb *be* as an auxiliary verb in the tense required *(was)*; c) follow with the **past participle** of the main verb *(eaten),* which must be a transitive verb of course, and, often optionally; d) end with *by* and the agent *(Mr Wolf).* Sometimes an instrument might (also) be mentioned, e.g *with a fork.*

The verb/-phrase changes from the active form *(ate)* to the **passive form** *(was eaten).*

> **the past participle** has two main contexts:
> 1. after the auxiliary *have* in perfect tenses;
> 2. after the verb *be* in passive sentences (transitive verbs only).

11.2 What do we teach?

In communicative language teaching we don't, of course, ask our students to carry out such grammatical gymnastics as in 11.1 above. Like much information in this book, this is for the teacher to know, to enable them to increase their professional knowledge and confidence, and to use in the required measure and at the required time. What do we teach? We teach use.

11.3 Uses of the passive

There are three major uses of the passive:

USE	EXAMPLE
1. To say what has happened to someone/something.	*Did you hear? Fido **was hit** by a car.* *All the crops **have been destroyed** (by locusts).*
2. To avoid mentioning the agent (the person doing the action), who is not required to be or cannot be made known.	*The matter **is being attended to**.* *The bridge **will be repaired**.*
3. To conform with normal English discourse, keeping the 'topic' (the 'old', the subject of the previous sentence, here *they)* at the front of the sentence, and the new information in the predicate.	*United played a lousy game ... in the end **they were crucified** (by Rovers).* (Compare: *Rovers wanted revenge ... in short, they crucified United.*)

Manufacturing processes, and crimes, are popular for practising the present and past passive:

> The barley **is roasted** ... the hops **are added** ...
> Maurizio Gucci and Gianni Versace **were murdered**.

And remember, this is not mathematics – some verbs, mostly stative, just don't 'work' in the passive:

> *?You are fitted by that suit*. *?The competition was entered by Joan.*

While others would sound strange in the active form:

> *?It flabbergasted me*. *?Your calls have inundated us.*

WANTED MAN JAILED

5'6"

5'0"

INT 21195XA-726
TPD 8612-43961

Fugitive James Sanders, who escaped from jail in 1975, (6) _____ in Texas after ringing the FBI to check if he was still on its wanted list.

STABBED IN THE BACK

Mr Clarence Ramsey (7) _____ seriously _____ yesterday when a man came up behind him and stabbed him in the back. Turning round to face his attacker, Mr Ramsey was

d) What are the advantages of using the passive? Match these reasons to the three sentences in 2.

1 The agent is unknown.
2 The agent is obvious.
3 You want to keep the important information at the beginning of the sentence.

4 Complete the short newspaper stories on the left with a suitable verb from the box.

| steal | handcuff | rescue | sentence | arrest | injure | kill |
| rob | damage | break | shoot | kill | find guilty | destroy |

5 What are the experiences of the class? Ask questions to find someone who:

- has been searched by customs.
- has been stopped for speeding.
- has been let down by a friend.
- has been photographed by a local newspaper.
- has been mistaken for somebody else.
- has been injured playing a sport.
- has been given a present they didn't like.
- has been interviewed on radio or television.
- has been questioned by the police.

From *Inside Out Intermediate* by S. Kay & V. Jones. (Macmillan) Past and present perfect passive.

11.4 *Get* instead of *be*

Get may be used instead of *be* in many cases. The first use in the table (informal/colloquial) generally applies across the board. Notice that most of these structures are **agentless passives**.

USE	EXAMPLE
1. in informal/colloquial communication	*You get told one thing, then another happens.*
2. to avoid ambiguity with the past participle as adjective (when the agent is not mentioned). The verb *be* is often followed by an adjective so *get* may be preferred for faster and more accurate communication.	*My bike was broken.* (Mine was a broken bike?) *He is beaten/embarrassed.* (Now or usually?) *My bike got broken.* (That's what happened.) *He gets beaten/embarrassed.* (Usually.)
3. often used for unfortunate/unexpected events	*She got ripped off. We got eaten alive by midges.*
4. as *get* is often a synonym of *become* it therefore can carry its 'change over time' meaning.	*The papers got destroyed by the rain. We got drenched.*
5. an achievement, usually after time/effort	*She (finally) got picked for the job.*

11.5 Passive in tenses

Task 11.1 Fill in the right hand column with the passive transformations. The first one has been done for you. The future continuous and perfect continuous forms are rarely used, but two examples are shown for those who may be interested (marked with an 'R').

TENSE (etc.)	ACTIVE	PASSIVE
present simple	*She takes photos.*	*Photos are taken by her.*
present continuous	*She is taking photos.*	
past simple	*She took a photo.*	
past continuous	*She was taking a photo.*	
future simple	*She'll take a photo.*	
future with *going to*	*She's going to take a photo.*	
(future continuous)	*She'll be taking photos.*	*Photos will be being taken by her.* [R]
present perfect simple	*She has taken a decision.*	
(present perfect cont.)	*She has been taking photos.*	*Photos have been being taken by her.* [R]
past perfect simple	*She had taken photos before then.*	
future perfect simple	*She will have mastered relative clauses by next week.*	
modal	*Someone might buy it.*	
modal perfect	*Someone could have killed us.*	
infinitive (or gerund)	*Someone needs to clean my desk.*	
perfect infinitive	*Better to have loved.*	
gerund (of *be*)	*He doesn't like it when someone tells him what to do.*	(Don't use *it*.)

11.6 Causative passive

Using *have* or *get* we say how we cause something to be done, or experience some misfortune:

[1] *She had/got her hair done last Friday.*
[2] *She had her wallet stolen.*
[3] *She got her wallet stolen.*
[4] *She got the kids dressed.*
[5] *I'll have you thrown out.*
[6] *He'll get us thrown out.*
[7] *Did he get that leak fixed?*

Where the context is a normal chore, as in *I'm going to have/get the car repaired* or [1] above, there seems to be a free choice of *have* or *get*. But in other situations each appears to carry a certain connotation. Become aware of these through the task below.

Task 11.2 Referring to the list of sentences above,

    a) Which implies irresponsibility?
    b) Which is preferred for a threat?
    c) Which implies misfortune?
    d) Which implies that the 'misfortune' was arranged?
    e) Which may imply some delay/effort?
    f) Which is the odd-one-out and why?

For more on causatives see 13.10.1 and 20.4.1.

11.7 Direct and indirect object

Not until they reach upper-intermediate or advanced level would students be able to produce confidently passive structures with verbs that take two objects. A section of 1.13 is reproduced here as a reminder of these:

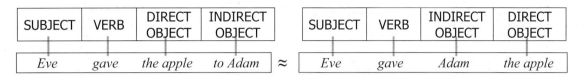

SUBJECT	VERB	DIRECT OBJECT	INDIRECT OBJECT		SUBJECT	VERB	INDIRECT OBJECT	DIRECT OBJECT
Eve	gave	the apple	to Adam	≈	Eve	gave	Adam	the apple

Depending on 'topic fronting' (see 11.3) the passive form of the above could be either

| *The apple was given to Adam (by Eve).* | or | *Adam was given the apple (by Eve).* |

Write these sentences in another way, beginning in the way shown.

1 They didn't give me the information I needed.
   I *wasn't given the information I needed.*

2 They asked me some difficult questions at the interview.
   I ....

3 Linda's colleagues gave her a present when she retired.
   Linda ....

4 Nobody told me about the meeting.
   I wasn't ....

5 How much will they pay you for your work?
   How much will you ....

6 I think they should have offered Tom the job.
   I think Tom ....

7 Has anybody shown you what to do?
   Have you ....

From *English Grammar in Use* by R. Murphy (CUP). Passives with ditransitive verbs.

Task 11.3 In the extract above the first sentence could also transform as *The information I needed wasn't given (to) me,* where the 'thing', the direct object, rather than the person, may come first.

Also look at sentences 4 and 7 above and suggest why such a transformation is unacceptable in these cases.

11.8 *It is said,* etc.

We can say *People say/believe/think/argue/understand that* ... but for a more formal register we may use the preparatory subject *it* and the passive form of these reporting verbs:

   [1] *It is said that prostitution is the oldest profession.*
   [2] *It is said that Leonardo invented the helicopter.*

Often the subject can be fronted; the past participle is then followed by the infinitive:

   [1a] *Prostitution is said to be the oldest profession.*
   [2a] *Leonardo is said to have invented the helicopter.*

12 Irregular verbs

Regular verbs form their past tense and past participle by adding -d or -ed. Verbs which form their past tense and/or past participle in other ways, e.g. with a vowel change, as in sing, sang, sung, or even with no change, as in cut, cut, cut, are irregular. A reasonably full list follows (AmE = American English alternative).

12.1 List of irregular verbs (page 1 of 2)

INFINITIVE	PAST TENSE	PAST PARTICIPLE
arise	arose	arisen
awake	awoke/AmE awaked	awoken/AmE awaked
be	was, were	been
bear	bore	borne
---	----	born (passive only)
beat	beat	beaten
become	became	become
beget	begot/begat	begotten/begot
begin	began	begun
bend	bent	bent
beseech	beseeched/besought	beseeched/besought
bet	bet/betted	bet/betted
bid (request)	bade/bid	bidden/bid
bid (auction)	bid	bid
bind	bound	bound
bite	bit	bitten
bleed	bled	bled
blow	blew	blown
break	broke	broken
breed	bred	bred
bring	brought	brought
broadcast	broadcast/AmE -ed	broadcast/AmE -ed
build	built	built
burn	burnt/burned	burnt/burned
burst	burst	burst
bust	bust/busted	bust/busted
buy	bought	bought
cast	cast	cast
catch	caught	caught
choose	chose	chosen
cleave (split)	cleaved/cleft/clove	cleaved/cleft/cloven
cleave (adhere)	cleaved/clove	cleaved
cling	clung	clung
come	came	come
cost	cost	cost
creep	crept	crept
cut	cut	cut
deal	dealt	dealt
dig	dug	dug
dive	dived/AmE dove	dived/AmE dove
do	did	done
draw	drew	drawn
dream	dreamt/dreamed	dreamt/dreamed
drink	drank	drunk
drive	drove	driven
dwell	dwelt/AmE dwelled	dwelt/AmE dwelled
eat	ate	eaten
fall	fell	fallen
feed	fed	fed
feel	felt	felt
fight	fought	fought
find	found	found
fit	fitted/fit	fitted/fit
flee	fled	fled
fling	flung	flung
fly	flew	flown
forbid	forbade/AmE forbad	forbidden
forecast	forecast/-ed	forecast/-ed
forget	forgot	forgotten/AmE forgot
forgive	forgave	forgiven
forsake	forsook	forsaken
freeze	froze	frozen
get	got	got/AmE gotten
give	gave	given
go	went	gone
grind	ground	ground
grow	grew	grown
hang	hung	hung
hang (execute)[R]	hanged	hanged
have	had	had
hear	heard	heard
heave[R]	heaved	heaved
heave (in)to (naut.)	hove	hove
hide	hid	hidden
hit	hit	hit
hold	held	held
hurt	hurt	hurt
keep	kept	kept
kneel	knelt/AmE kneeled	knelt/AmE kneeled
knit (pref. garments)	knit/knitted	knit/knitted
knit (pref. bones)	knit	knit
know	knew	known
lay	laid	laid

12.1 List of irregular verbs (page 2 of 2)

INFINITIVE	PAST TENSE	PAST PARTICIPLE
lead	led	led
lean	leant/leaned	leant/leaned
leap	leapt/leaped	leapt/leaped
learn	learnt/learned	learnt/learned
leave	left	left
lend	lent	lent
let	let	let
lie (down)	lay	lain
light	lit/lighted	lit/lighted
lose	lost	lost
make	made	made
mean	meant	meant
meet	met	met
mistake	mistook	mistaken
mow	mowed	mown/mowed
pay	paid	paid
plead	pleaded/*AmE* pled	pleaded/*AmE* pled
prove	proved	proved/proven
put	put	put
quit	quit/quitted	quit/quitted
read	read	read
rid	rid	rid
ride	rode	ridden
ring	rang	rung
rise	rose	risen
run	ran	run
saw	sawed	sawn/*AmE* sawed
say	said	said
see	saw	seen
seek	sought	sought
sell	sold	sold
send	sent	sent
set	set	set
sew	sewed	sewn/sewed
shake	shook	shaken
shear	sheared	shorn/sheared
shed	shed	shed
shine (a light)	shone	shone
shine (polish) R	shined	shined
shit	shit/-ted/shat	shit/-ted/shat
shoe	shod	shod
shoot	shot	shot
show	showed	shown/showed
shrink	shrank/shrunk	shrunk/*AmE* shrunken
shut	shut	shut
sing	sang	sung
sink	sank	sunk
sit	sat	sat
slay	slew	slewn
sleep	slept	slept
slide	slid	slid
sling	slung	slung
slink	slunk	slunk
slit	slit	slit
smell	smelt/smelled	smelt/smelled
smite	smote	smitten
sow	sowed	sown/sowed
speak	spoke	spoken
speed	sped/speeded	sped/speeded
spell	spelt/spelled	spelt/spelled
spend	spent	spent
spill	spilt/spilled	spilt/spilled
spin	spun	spun
spit	spat/spit	spat/spit
split	split	split
spoil	spoilt/spoiled	spoilt/spoiled
spread	spread	spread
spring	sprang	sprung
stand	stood	stood
steal	stole	stolen
stick	stuck	stuck
sting	stung	stung
stink	stank/stunk	stunk
stride	strode	stridden, strode
strike	struck	struck
string	strung	strung
strive	strove, strived	striven, strived
swear	swore	sworn
sweep	swept	swept
swell	swelled	swollen/swelled
swim	swam	swum
swing	swung	swung
take	took	taken
teach	taught	taught
tear	tore	torn
tell	told	told
think	thought	thought
thrive	thrived/*AmE* throve	thrived/*AmE* thriven
throw	threw	thrown
thrust	thrust	thrust
tread	trod/*AmE* treaded	trodden/trod
wake (up)	woke/*AmE* waked	woken/*AmE* waked
wake (corpse) R	waked	waked
wear	wore	worn
weave (carpet)	wove	woven
weave (in traffic) R	weaved	weaved
wed	wedded/wed	wedded/wed
weep	wept	wept
wet	wet/wetted	wet/wetted
win	won	won
wind (wrap)	wound/*AmE* winded	wound/*AmE* winded
wring	wrung	wrung
write	wrote	written

12.2 About the list

1. Five regular verbs (marked [R]) are included for comparison purposes.
2. *Become* is a derivative of *come* and is included as an example for *forego, outbid, underlay,* etc.
3. *Cleave* is little used now but is included as an example of a 'minefield' with archaic forms. *Cloven* is used only in *cloven hoof,* a compound noun, or *cloven hoofed,* a compound adjective. For the second entry (= adhere) the Oxford Advanced Learner's Dictionary includes the options *cleft/clove* and *cleft/cloven* as in the first, and has a further regular entry for = remain loyal or believing.
4. Alternatives of extremely low frequency are underlined with a dotted line.
5. Many speakers accept *hung* as the past tense and past participle for *hang* in the sense 'execute'.
6. Data from the *Oxford Advanced Learner's Dictionary, Merriam-Webster's Collegiate Dictionary* and various corpora.

12.3 Native speaker errors

Native speakers break grammar rules every day, influenced by some analogy:

>*I should've went earlier;* *I would've took that road;*

or the sound, e.g. where 'drunk' has a negative connotation:

>*I've only drank two;*

or a half-way house, e.g. between present perfect and past simple:

>*I seen it.*

These are just instances of the tendency for language to change. In general, some irregular past tense forms will tend to be 'regularised' or follow some analogy.

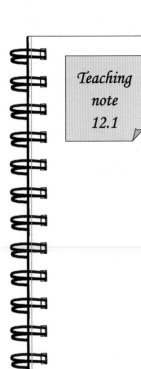

Teaching note 12.1

Lists of irregular verbs are contained in all grammar books because students (and teachers!) need to refer to them often. Some students endeavour to learn the most common irregular verbs off by heart, but an unbalanced diet of irregular verbs is not recommended. Most learners acquire them the same way native speakers do – by constantly coming across them in communicative contexts.

For a review exercise, get a relevant, not too difficult text (don't forget the free lessons on the internet). Blank out the appropriate verbs. If any of these are difficult to guess leave the first letter or two visible. Photocopy (zoom up newspaper text a little for easier reading) and distribute. Let students work in pairs to fill in the correct verb foms. Check around.

As a follow-on, students could write their own narratives (help by going round, correcting and encouraging) and read them out in small groups. When students settle down at the task, and the situation allows, you should endeavour to write your own contribution also. Show it on the OHP or the board.

When doing/requesting a check many teachers and students just say "one – two - three" or "take - took - taken" etc, as "infinitive/base - past tense - past participle" is quite a mouthful.

13 Modal auxiliary verbs

13.1 Auxiliary verbs

There are two types of auxiliary verbs: **primary auxiliary verbs**, which comprise *be* (1.5), *have* (3.1.1) and *do* (questions, negatives and emphasis); and the **modal auxiliary verbs** *(can, may, will, should,* etc.*)*. Modal auxiliary verbs are also called modal auxiliaries, modal verbs or modals.

13.2 Definition/function of modals

Modal auxiliaries are followed by (one or more primary aux. verbs and) a main verb (except in the case of inversion, etc.). Unlike the primary auxiliaries *(be, have* and *do)* which mainly have a grammatical function, the modal auxiliaries carry meaning. Although it is an overly strong definition of function you may as a mnemonic interpret *modal* as 'conveying the *mood* or opinion of the speaker', e.g. expressing ability, obligation, advice, possibility, etc.

 Remember: the auxiliary verb always carries the tense, even though with most modals it is not visible. A common error is:

 He **can clean̲s̲ his room.*

13.3 List of modals

The following list is of my own construction. Among grammarians there is not full agreement on the terminology/categorization.

MODALS (SIMPLE MODALS)	*can* *could*	*may* *might*	*will* *would*	*shall* *should*	*ought to* *must*	
SEMI-MODALS	*need*	*dare*	*used to*		*have (got) to*	
PHRASAL MODALS	*had better* *may as well* *might as well* *would rather*	*be +* { *able to, about to, allowed to, apt to, bound to, certain to, due to, going to, liable to, likely to, meant to, supposed to, sure to*				*be to*

13.4 Structure of (simple) modals

Modals are not inflected, i.e. there is no *-ed* for past tense, no *-s* for third person singular present and no preceding *do*. The optional contraction of the negative (which doesn't apply to *may*) is common in informal registers.

 Modals are followed by the bare infinitive (infinitive without *to*), so the modal itself carries the tense, although it is not inflected. *Ought* is usually followed by *to*, then justifying relegation to semi-modal status, but in ELT *ought to* is treated equally with *should,* etc, as a modal.

13.5 Uses of (simple) modals

Modals are quite versatile in the meanings they convey. For example, *could* has the functions of asking permission, asking for assistance, making requests, expressing ability in the past, expressing possibility, making suggestions. There are also some synonyms, e.g. *can = may = could* in the function of requesting permission, the choice of modal decided mainly by register.

Task 13.1 Match the examples below with the uses on the next page. The first one has been done. For *will* and *shall* see 4.1.

MODAL	EXAMPLE
can('t)	1. _c_ I can teach adults, I can't teach kids. I can('t) meet you at nine. 2. ___ Can I borrow your husband for a while? 3. ___ She's had four helpings; she can't still be hungry! 4. ___ I can('t) hear your heartbeat. 5. ___ It can swing around without any warning.
could(n't)	1. ___ He could play the piano before he could read. 2. ___ Could you please stop calling me Al? 3. ___ It could't be Linda; she's in Stockholm. 4. ___ Could that be Helga now? 5. ___ We could always go by Shank's pony.
may (not)	1. ___ May I leave the room/have some watermelon? 2. ___ It may well be the end of civilization as we know it. 3. ___ May the road rise with you. 4. ___ I *may* be an oldie, but I'm a goodie too.
might(n't)	1. ___ He mightn't recognize her. 2. ___ You might drop in on old Jim as you're passing. 3. ___ I just *might* be tempted.
would(n't)	1. ___ Would you like me to show you around? 2. ___ Would you please be quiet? 3. ___ It wouldn't be pasteurised, of course, but we loved it. 4. ___ She *would* say that, wouldn't she – she's selling it. 5. ___ The marriage was arranged. She would soon leave her family.
should(n't)	1. ___ Passengers wishing to disembark should go to the purser's office. 2. ___ People who live in glasshouses shouldn't throw stones. 3. ___ It should work now. 4. ___ I should like to see that report. 5. ___ Funny that you should think so.
ought(n't) to	1. ___ You ought to have consulted me. There ought to be a law against it. 2. ___ You ought to have more respect. 3. ___ That ought to do the trick. They ought to be here by now.
must(n't)	1. ___ We really must be going now. 2. ___ You really *must* stay for dinner next time. 3. ___ You must never see her again. You mustn't tell a soul. 4. ___ *Must* you leave your socks there? 5. ___ He hasn't touched it; he must still be pining for her.

MODAL	USES
can('t)	a) requesting/granting/refusing sthg/permission b) expressing surprise, disbelief / negative deduction c) expressing (in)ability / making future arrangements d) expressing tendency e) expressing perception or lack thereof (mainly BrE)
could(n't)	a) suggesting b) requesting sthg/permission (register varies with intonation, etc.) c) expressing past (in)ability d) expressing impossibility/surprise/conviction. / Negative deduction e) expressing/questioning possibility - past of *can* and *may* (most uses) in reported speech – see 13.9.2. Also see chapter 19.
may (not)	a) wishing/cursing b) requesting/granting/refusing permission (slightly more formal than *can*) c) expressing possibility d) conceding (often stressed)
might(n't)	a) expressing/questioning possibility b) commonly collocating with this focusing adverb to express slight possibility (often stressed) c) making a tentative request - past of *may* (usually possibility) in reported speech – see 13.9.2. Also see chapter 19.
would(n't)	a) (stressed) commenting on predictability of sbdy's past action b) offering sthg. (declarative: expressing desire/request) c) habitual event/repeated state in the past (see 13.7.2) d) requesting/commanding (affirmative) e) future in the past - For *would* as past of *will/shall* in reported speech see 13.9.2, also 17.2 For *would* in conditional sentences see chapter 19.
should(n't)	a) expressing desire for sthg. (BrE) b) expressing obligation c) advising d) in certain *that* clauses e) expressing logical expectation - (*Should* is not the past of *shall* to any extent in ELT.) Also see chapter 19.
ought(n't) to	a) expressing logical expectation b) expressing (moral) obligation/duty/requirement (not so formal as *should*) c) advising
must(n't)	a) (stressed) rhetorical question implying disapproval b) deducing the cause of/reason for sthg. c) (stressed) firm invitation/recommendation d) expressing 'internal' obligation (sometimes stressed) e) commanding or advising strongly

13.6 'Deduction' modals

Almost all of the functions of modals have been shown in task 13.1. But because the function of 'deduction/probability' is the basis of many coursebook lessons we include a reminder of it below in diagrammatic form. When we express our assessment of the possibility/probability of a situation/event we usually use these modals (for *will* see 4.1):

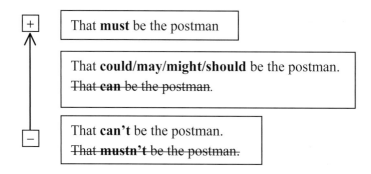

13.7 Semi-modals

SEMI-MODALS	*need*	*dare*	*used to*	*have (got) to*

13.7.1 *Need* and *dare*

Need and *dare* operate as modals when followed by the bare infinitive, and as main verbs when followed by the full infinitive, then undergoing any inflection (tense, 3rd person -*s* marking).

 Dare can undergo some inflection while remaining a modal.

 Need and *dare* as modals usually only appear in [1] negative statements and [2] affirmative questions; *dare* also appears in [3] negative imperatives:

    [1] *You **needn't** finish that tonight.* [2] ***Need** you ask?*
    [1a] *I **daren't** ask. She didn't **dare** (to) tell him.* [2a] ***Dare** I ask?*
    [3] *Don't you **dare** tell him!*

Task 13.2

1. Explain the error in **You needn't a visa.*
2. Which of the two sentences below expresses general (non-)requirement?. Which expresses a more immediate (non-)requirement? Suggest a suitable situation and a following 'reason' sentence in an imagined dialogue for each.
   a) *You needn't lock your car.*
   b) *You don't need to lock your car.*

13.7.2 *Used to* and *would* – functions

Used to and *would* describe past habitual actions/states (strongly implying that these have ceased). *Used to* often introduces a topic and *would* often follows it up:

> TOPIC: Sue **used to** live in Torquay. She **used to** take family photos in people's homes.
> FOLLOW UP: Every day she **would** drive to a house and set up her equipment.

There is another functional difference which is revealed on carrying out the task below.

Task 13.3 Complete the table below by writing *habitual action in the past* and *durative state in the past* in the appropriate blank cells a) and b).

'TENSE'	EXAMPLE	USE
used to	*She used to /~~would~~ live in Torquay.* *She used to /~~would~~ like driving.*	a)
used to/would	*She used to /would drive to a house.* *She used to /would set up her equipment in the house.*	b)

Would can convey temporary repeated states but not durative/permanent states. Compare:

> *She would live in Torquay for 6 months, London for another 6 and then back to Torquay again.*
> **She would live in Torquay but I don't know where she moved to.*

13.7.3 *Used to* – forms

There is a choice of forms for *used to* in the negative and interrogative:

> *She didn't use to; she use(d)n't to; she used not to; (she never used to).*
> *Did she use to? Used she to?*

The spellings *She didn't used to* and *Did she used to* used to be acceptable but are now considered archaic.

Teaching note 13.1

When the context is clear the past simple may be used instead of *used to*, e.g. *I smoked when I was a kid; the Aztecs offered human sacrifice*.

Used to is usually presented at elementary and pre-intermediate levels; *would* (for past habitual actions) is left till later. Actually, for past habits English speakers use *would* much more than *used to** but as *would* has many more uses it would cause greater learning difficulty. Furthermore, the topic introduction (*used to*) is sufficient at elementary level as the learner would not have the linguistic ability to follow up in any detail.

On the learning path students may avoid *used to* for some time as it resembles the main verb *use* as in *used for,* etc. However, as they get more comfortable with it listen out for errors like **He uses to eat cornflakes now* for the intended *He usually eats cornflakes now,* and later **I am used to drive on the left now* for the intended *I am used to driving on the left now*.

Don't present, e.g. *I am used to teaching,* i.e. the adjective *used* + preposition *to* + gerund (-ing form) in comparison with this *used to* (semi-modal aux. verb including infinitive particle) unless students request it and are at the level to handle it!

Negative *I didn't use to* and interrogative *Did you use to?* forms are not often used, so there's no need to dwell on them.

*Willis, D. & J. "Analytic techniques to help students learn grammar" in *Creativity in Language Teaching*. British Council 1988.

3 Practice

Make sentences which introduce a topic by matching the beginnings 1-9 to the endings a-i.

1. When I was a kid, I used to play
2. When I was younger, I used to go
3. When I was about twelve or thirteen, I used to collect
4. When I was at primary school, I used to love
5. When I was about eight or nine, I used to have this
6. When I was at school, I used to get into
7. When I was a boy, I used to spend a lot of
8. I used to be a lot more impatient
9. I used to make

a. lots of mistakes when I first started learning Spanish.
b. than I am now.
c. time down on the beach near my house.
d. the piano.
e. stamps.
f. trouble all the time.
g. fishing at the weekends in this river near my house.
h. painting.
i. great friend called Matt.

Now match the follow-up comments I-ix to the sentences 1-9 in Exercise 3 on page 124.

i. I'd be rude to teachers or I'd be late, and I'd end up having to go and see the headmaster!
ii. I'd lose my temper at the smallest thing and I'd get really annoyed if I ever had to wait for things! I was horrible!
iii. I'd have lessons every week, and I'd practise at home, but eventually I got bored with it.
iv. I'd try to catch crabs and collect shells and I'd sometimes go swimming as well. It was great!
v. I'd get words mixed up and speak bits of French by mistake and forget things! It was awful!
vi. We'd spend all our time together and we'd go skate-boarding, climb trees and things like that.
vii. I'd buy them from a shop near my house and steam them off old envelopes.
viii. I'd do funny little portraits and trees and landscapes

5 Free practice

Now think of three things you used to do when you were younger. Write a bit about them.

1. When I was ...., I used to ....
   I'd .... and I'd ....

From *Innovations Intermediate* by H. Deller & A. Walkley with D. Hocking. © 2004 Reprinted with permission of Heinle, a division of Thomson Learning. *Used to* and *would* .

13.7.4 Difficulties with *must* and *have (got) to*

Have to is fully inflected but as it functions (in the past) as the past of *must* it is slotted into the semi-modal category. German L1 students will tend to over-use *must*, others will travel the normal learning curve until the main differences in meaning are felt. That being said, the incidences where the wrong choice would cause communication breakdown are few. The main differences in usage are outlined below.

Briefly, *must* expresses internal obligation, e.g. *I/we **must** remember to go to the optician's;*
have to expresses external obligation, e.g. *I/we **have to** start wearing glasses.*

In AmE *have got to* (usually pronounced *gotta*) is often preferred over *have to* or *must*.

A command can be seen as an appeal for some sort of internal obligation on the listener's part. The power relationship of speaker to listener (register) is important (*have to* is also possible):

*You **must** be home by midnight.*

*You really **must** leave now, darling.*

The unacceptability of *haven't to* as an imperative results in a high frequency of *mustn't*:

*You **mustn't** be home late. You ~~haven't to~~ be home late. You **mustn't** tell a soul.*

Must is also often used in written instructions, or as a formal statement of a rule:

*All candidates **must** carry valid identification.*

6 Practice

Complete these sentences with must, mustn't, have to, or don't have to.

1. There's a funny noise coming from my car. I really .... take it in to the garage.
2. You really .... be late again. If you are, you might find yourself looking for another job!
3. Thank goodness I .... write in English at work! My spelling is awful.
4. The flight's at ten, and we .... check-in at least ninety minutes before.
5. If you get the chance, you really .... go and see the Van Gogh museum while you're in Amsterdam.
6. We're having a leaving party for Anne-Marie and we want it to be a surprise, so you .... tell her, whatever you do.
7. We .... be at the hotel by 9.30. Otherwise, the coach will leave without us.
8. I really .... make an appointment at the dentist's. It's over six months since I last went.

4 Had to/didn't have to

Put these sentences into the past.

1. I must be at the station by 6.30 tomorrow morning
   I .... this morning.
2. I don't have to be home early today.
   I .... yesterday.
3. I have to have a word with my boss later.
   I .... last week.
4. We must get our passports renewed.
   We .... last summer.
5. We have to get a taxi.
   We .... last night.
6. I must e-mail the report by twelve.
   I .... this morning.
7. We don't have to stay till the end,
   The meeting didn't finish until eleven, but we
   ....
8. I must pay my phone bill this week or I'll be cut off.
   I .... last week before they cut me off.

From *Innovations Intermediate* by H. Deller & A. Walkley with D. Hocking. © 2004 Reprinted with permission of Heinle, a division of Thomson Learning. *Must, have to* and *had to,* modals of obligation.

Task 13.4

1. Do task 6 from *Innovations Intermediate* above.
2. State the use of each modal (see 13.7.4 and task 13.1).

13.8 Phrasal modals

PHRASAL MODALS	had better may as well might as well would rather	be +	able to, about to, allowed to, apt to, bound to, certain to, due to, going to, liable to, likely to, meant to, supposed to, sure to	be to

Also called **periphrastic modals**, these each don't have such a range of meaning as the simple modals (thankfully for our students) although some are idiomatic, e.g. *liable* or *sure* are not as readily understood as *able* in

She **is able to** meet him; she **is liable to** meet him; she **is sure to** meet him.

Had better is used for advice, but with the register of authority or urgency (or humour in close relationships). It is pronounced as *you'd better* or *you better,* but the latter isn't regarded as correct in written English.

A reminder that obscure grammatical categories such as semi-modals and phrasal modals are not intended for the general ESOL classroom. Please read the introduction to this book.

13.8.1 *Be to*

You **are to** clean up after you.   – instruction usually to children
We **are to** be there by five.   – expectation/obligation

The use of *be to* in the past is sometimes called a 'future in the past':

We **were to** clean up after us.

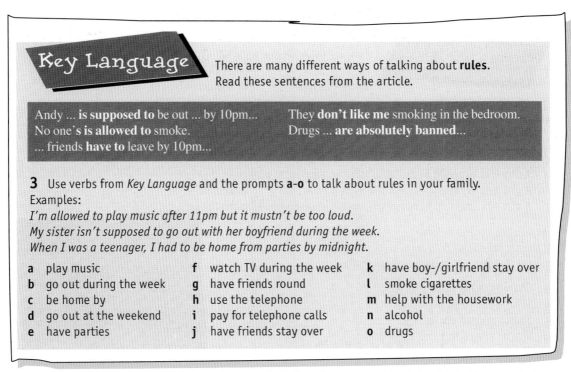

Key Language There are many different ways of talking about **rules**. Read these sentences from the article.

Andy ... **is supposed to** be out ... by 10pm...
No one's **is allowed to** smoke.
... friends **have to** leave by 10pm...

They **don't like me** smoking in the bedroom.
Drugs ... **are absolutely banned**...

3 Use verbs from *Key Language* and the prompts **a-o** to talk about rules in your family.
Examples:
I'm allowed to play music after 11pm but it mustn't be too loud.
My sister isn't supposed to go out with her boyfriend during the week.
When I was a teenager, I had to be home from parties by midnight.

a play music	**f** watch TV during the week	**k** have boy-/girlfriend stay over
b go out during the week	**g** have friends round	**l** smoke cigarettes
c be home by	**h** use the telephone	**m** help with the housework
d go out at the weekend	**i** pay for telephone calls	**n** alcohol
e have parties	**j** have friends stay over	**o** drugs

From *Ideas & Issues Intermediate* by O. Johnston & M. Farrell (Chancerel). Modals of obligation, permission. Also forms of disapproval. (For *don't like* + object pronoun + *-ing* see 7.2.3.)

13.9 Other past time contexts

13.9.1 In a main clause

We have seen that *could*, (ability in past) and *would* (habitual action in past) can contain past tense in their own forms. *Had to* usually serves as the past tense of *must*:

> *I **could/would/had to** play the piano when no one was around.*

(*Was able to* is often used instead of *could* for accomplishments, more temporary skills or situations.)

13.9.2 In a reported speech clause

Could and *would* also function in the past in reported (indirect) speech, corresponding to *can/may* (permission) and *will/shall* respectively:

DIRECT	REPORTED
You can/may dance.	*You said (that) we **could** dance*
I will/shall dance.	*She said (that) she **would** dance.*

Might functions in the past only in reported speech, corresponding to *may* or *might*. It is also interchangeable with *could* in this regard (all denoting possibility):

It may/might/could rain.	*We were advised (that) it **might/could** rain.*

Should, must, ought to, needn't and *daren't* can also operate in the past, but again only in reported speech/thought:

> *He knew (that) he **should/must/ought to/needn't/daren't** tell her.*

13.10 Modal perfect (modal + *have* for past time)

When a modal is followed by the perfect, e.g. *might have flown,* it is often called the **modal perfect**, although in ELT the 'modal + *have* for past time' will get a better reception.

The modal perfect is used to express possibility, obligation, deduction, assumption, etc, about something in the past. In that respect there is a relationship with the non-perfect form, but there are some difficulties:

> You **mustn't/shouldn't** cross the road there; you **could** be killed.
> You ~~**mustn't have**~~/**shouldn't have** crossed the road there; you **could have** been killed.

In AmE *must not* or *mustn't* are sometimes used instead of *can't* for negative deduction:

> BrE: *He's not heading for the departure gate – he **can't** have heard the announcement.*
> AmE: *He's not heading for the departure gate – he **must not** have heard the announcement.*

---

9 | Grammar in context

Complete the responses in these dialogues using must or must've.

1. A: My brother and his wife have actually got eleven kids now.
   B: Eleven! ....

2. A: We stayed in this huge twenty-storey hotel.
   B: Oh, one of those places! ....

3. A: I usually cycle into work, if it's not raining.
   B: Oh really? ....

4. A: I got up at five, just as the sun was coming up, and went for a walk along by the river.
   B: Wonderful! ....

5. A: I like my job, but I have to work a six-day week every week!
   B: Every week? ....

6. A: The plane was delayed forty-eight hours! Can you imagine what it was like?
   B: Forty-eight hours! ....

7. A: Did you hear that over 200 people were killed in that crash?
   B: I know. ....

From *Innovations Upper Intermediate* by H. Deller & D. Hocking, with A. Walkley. © 2004 Reprinted with permission of Heinle, a division of Thomson Learning. *Must* as modal of deduction.

13.10.1 Possible confusion with causative *have*

There may well be difficulty in differentiating between e.g. *must have* + past participle (deduction) and *must* (command) + *have/get* (causative) + object + past participle. Compare:

> [1] *You must have washed the car.* (deduction – *have* unstressed)
> [2] *You must have/get the car washed.* (command + causative – *have* stressed normally)

Obviously *get* seems the better option in [2] for a clearer difference, but we must remember that *get* is no friend of the learner's (2½ pages of entries in the Oxford Advanced Learner's Dictionary). Do <u>not</u> try to teach this causative until students want and are able to handle it. (See 11.6 and 20.4.1 for more on causatives.)

14 Phrasal verbs

14.1 Definition

A **phrasal verb** (or **multi-word verb**) is usually made up of a verb + adverb (e.g. *take off*).

It can also be made up of a verb + preposition (e.g. *look into...*). These may also be called **prepositional verbs**.

The adverb or preposition is often called a **particle**.

A **three-word phrasal verb** is a verb + adverb + preposition (e.g. *run out of...*).

What mainly distinguishes phrasal verbs from other verb + adverb/prep. phrases is that to varying extents their meaning is idiomatic, i.e. it cannot be deciphered from the separate parts. Some may have almost literal meaning (e.g. ***turn up*** *your collar*) but all would have semantic cohesion and many a one-word synonym. Semantic cohesion is shown by *look into* (=investigate) *the matter*, unlike *look into the room*, where *into the room* has more semantic cohesion. See type 3 below.

14.2 Types of phrasal verb

Most coursebooks present 4 types as shown below. Type 4a has been added here.

*He didn't **turn up**.*	TYPE 1: verb + adverb, intransitive
*He didn't **turn up** the radio /* *He didn't **turn** the radio/it **up**.*	TYPE 2: verb + adverb + object (transitive) (the verb and adverb are **separable**, allowing the object to come between them)
*He didn't **look into** the matter.*	TYPE 3: verb + preposition + object*
*(He didn't look **into the room**.)*	(verb + preposition + object* (not phrasal))
*He didn't **get away with** it.*	TYPE 4: verb + adv. + prep. + object*
*He didn't **let** me **in on** the secret.*	TYPE 4a: verb + obj. + adv. + prep. + object*

*object of the preposition, not verb; a preposition must be followed by a noun/-phrase or pronoun in the object case.

see off

From *Making Sense of Phrasal Verbs* by M. Shovel (ELB). Verb + adverb, transitive.

Task 14.1

> Formulate a rule based on your observation of the following:
>
> *I put the meeting off.   I put it off.   I put off the meeting.   *I put off it.*

14.3 Opacity

Below is a crude scale of opacity (unclearness, idiomaticness) of some phrasal verbs. Understandably it's this opacity that causes some difficulty, and often bemusement, for learners.

14.4 Adverb or preposition?

In many cases the same word can serve as an adverb or preposition. In [1] below, the phrasal verb is transitive, obliging it to take an object. This makes the structure appear identical with [2], which has an intransitive verb and a preposition phrase:

> [1] *He gave up the cigarettes.*
> [2] *He walked up the street.* (non-phrasal)

The real preposition phrase can be revealed by **fronting**, i.e. moving an item to the front of a sentence; this can be done with adverbials (incl. preposition phrases) of movement:

> [1a] **Up the cigarettes he gave.*
> [2a] *Up the street he walked.*

Obviously *up the cigarettes* is not a preposition phrase in this instance, and *up* is therefore not a preposition but an adverb, coupled with *gave*.

With a *phrasal* verb made up of a verb + preposition the collocation/cohesion may be too tight or the preposition too abstract to allow of such fronting:

> [3] *Into the room he looked.* (non-phrasal)
> [4] *?Into the matter he looked.*
> [5] **After the children she looked.*

Thankfully there are a few words that keep to their word class, e.g *apart* is always an adverb and *from* is always a preposition.

Among the most common adverbs are *up, down, on, off,* conveying notions of completion, increase/decrease, continuation, departure:

> *drink up   knock it down   carry on   make off with*

Task 14.2

> 1. Which of the phrasal verbs below is intransitive?
> 2. Which undergoes a change of meaning when a certain object comes between the verb and particle?
> 3. Which sentence contains a verb + preposition with literal meaning (non-phrasal)?
>
>   a) *He saw it through.*
>   b) *The deal fell through.*
>   c) *It fell through the skylight.*
>   d) *He saw through her scheme.*

Students occasionally ask for lessons devoted to phrasal verbs. It's as well to point out to them that they have been learning phrasal verbs from elementary level relatively effortlessly. It would be hard to get through such a level without learning "What time do you <u>get up</u>?", "She has to <u>look after</u> the children", even "Please <u>look</u> it <u>up</u> in your dictionary", etc.

Teaching note 14.1

Lest any teacher forget, the best way to learn a language is by listening, reading and speaking (and writing) in communicative contexts, with all the visual assistance and encouragement required. It certainly worked in learning our L1 (first language). This is not to rule out practice and revision exercises; students are often intrigued at the challenge involved in choosing the correct phrasal verb for gap-filling etc, but try not to overstay your welcome on such 'contolled practice' exercises.

14.4 Pronunciation – stress placement

With verb + adverb [1] the primary stress falls on the adverb. With most verb + prepositions [2a] the primary stress usually falls on the verb, but there are some [2b] which behave like verb + adverb:

[1] *When are you going to call BACK?*

[2a] *When are you going to CALL on Greg?*   [2b] *Who's going to look AFTER you?*

With nouns formed from phrasal verbs the primary stress, as with most bisyllabic nouns, is on the first syllable:

[3] When is the TAKEover going ahead?

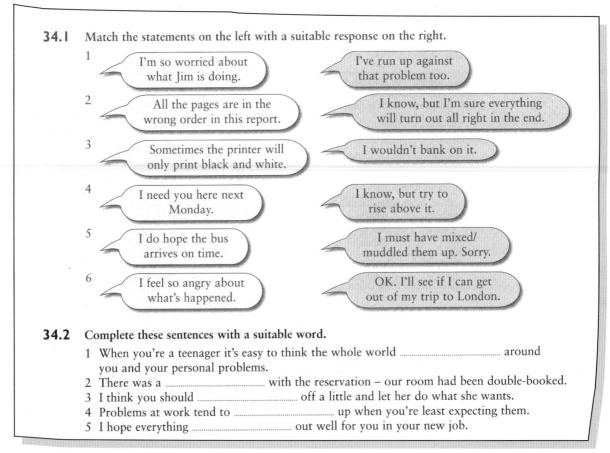

34.1   Match the statements on the left with a suitable response on the right.

1   I'm so worried about what Jim is doing.
I've run up against that problem too.

2   All the pages are in the wrong order in this report.
I know, but I'm sure everything will turn out all right in the end.

3   Sometimes the printer will only print black and white.
I wouldn't bank on it.

4   I need you here next Monday.
I know, but try to rise above it.

5   I do hope the bus arrives on time.
I must have mixed/ muddled them up. Sorry.

6   I feel so angry about what's happened.
OK. I'll see if I can get out of my trip to London.

34.2   Complete these sentences with a suitable word.

1   When you're a teenager it's easy to think the whole world .... around you and your personal problems.

2   There was a .... with the reservation – our room had been double-booked.

3   I think you should .... off a little and let her do what she wants.

4   Problems at work tend to .... up when you're least expecting them.

5   I hope everything .... out well for you in your new job.

From *English Phrasal Verbs in Use* by M. McCarthy & F. O'Dell (CUP). Phrasal verbs for (problem) situations.

15 Questions

15.1 Types and form

Task 15.1 Two of the rows below are mismatched. Match them correctly.

TYPE OF QUESTION	EXAMPLE
1. **Yes/no question** with verb *be*	a) *Are you in Amnesty International?*
2. **Yes/no question** with modal aux. verb	b) *Can you smell the lilac?*
3. **Yes/no question** with primary aux. verb	c) *Do you eat snails? Have they gone?*
4. **Wh-question**, the wh- word being the object	d) *Who(m) can she go with?*
5. **Wh- question**, the wh- word being the subject	e) *What goes 'zzub zzub'?*
6. **Tag question** with primary aux. verb	f) *You wouldn't tell, would you?*
7. **Tag question** with modal aux. verb	g) *You liked Sinéad, didn't you?*

Yes/no questions are probably the first type that students acquire, mostly using the verb *be*. As a practice activity a game of '20 questions' or 'What's my job/hobby?' can be effective.

The **'dummy' auxiliary *do*** is brought into service to form questions (and negatives) in English if the verb is not *be* or there is no other auxiliary verb in the structure (see 23.1).

Wh- questions even include questions starting with *how*. Teachers ask so many questions that good input is contained in everyday classroom language. For free practice, information-gap activities such as Spot the Difference and Describe and Draw are effective.

Tag questions are perhaps the last type of question that is acquired, being a little difficult in structure and being inessential in communicating facts. Tag questions seek confirmation or agreement, or are used for reproach, humour, etc. The distinction is carried by rising or falling intonation.

Inversion (the reverse order of the subject and aux. verb – see 9.2.5) is a feature of all English direct questions, except when the wh- word is the subject of the sentence (type 5 above), or when the question is an **echo question**, e.g. *You eat snails?/You eat what?*

Task 15.2 Referring to the table above,
  1. Which type of wh-question does not require an aux. verb (apart from one with the verb *be*?
  2. What other wh-word can be used in type 5?

15.2 *Have you got* and *do you have*

These are used more or less equally, although *have got* is more informal. *Have got* is not the present perfect of *got*, but simply means *have*. Past tense forms of *have got*, e.g. **I had got enough money,* are not fully acceptable. Answers to the respective forms are usually *Yes I have* and *Yes I do*.

  Have you a pen? is acceptable but of low frequency, therefore not usually taught.

From *Grammar Games and Activities 1* by P. Watcyn-Jones (Penguin), illustrations © Bruce Hogarth (David Lewis Illustrations) 1995. Find the differences activity.

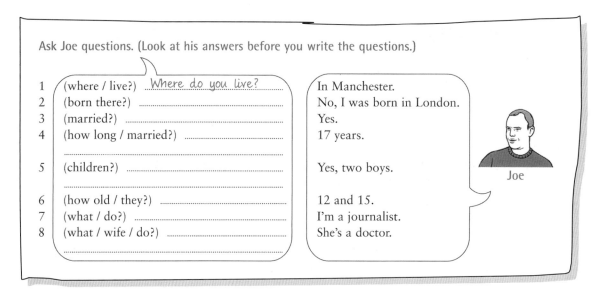

From *English Grammar in Use* by R. Murphy (CUP). Constructing questions from prompt words and answers.

33 Questions & answers

1 _____ is the sacred river of India?

2 _____ country is Mecca?

3 _____ is the GUM department store?

4 _____ wrote 'The Republic'?

5 _____ strings does a violin have?

6 _____ white horse was called 'Marengo'?

7 _____ film did Leonardo di Caprio freeze to death in the sea?

8 _____ is temperature measured?

9 _____ section of the orchestra does the drum belong?

From *Grammar Games and Activities 2* by D. Howard-Williams (Penguin). Gap-fill quiz (9 of 20 questions).

16 Clauses

16.1 Definition

When a sentence is itself made up of two or more sentences these sentences are called **clauses**. Clauses are identifiable by their having a verb (**non-finite clauses** contain a non-finite verb, i.e. an infinitive or participle, even a gerund, which is technically a noun of course).

16.2 Coordinate clauses

When the clauses in a sentence are of equal importance, each having a subject and predicate, they are called **coordinate clauses**. Coordinate clauses are joined by **coordinating conjunctions**, these being mainly *and, or* and *but:*

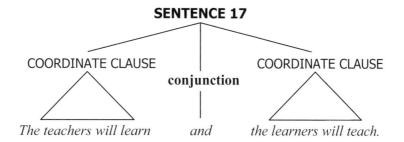

16.2.1 Ellipsis

Ellipsis (leaving out a word/words) commonly occurs across coordinate clauses:

> *The teachers will learn and the learners (will) teach ;*
> *I can surf but <u>she</u> can't (surf).*
> *Dave told the teachers but (Dave) forgot to inform the office staff.*
> *The office staff were irked by (his oversight) and reported his oversight.*

Colloquially, at the start of a sentence the subject (and aux. or *be* in questions) are often ellipted:

> *"Been to the show yet?"   "No, can't get tickets."*

16.3 Subordinate clauses

When there is a clause which could function as a noun, adjective or adverbial with or within a **main clause**, thus carrying information subordinate to that in the main clause, this clause is called a **subordinate clause**. A **complex sentence** is one composed of a main clause and one or more subordinate clauses.

A subordinate clause often starts with a **subordinating conjunction**, e.g.

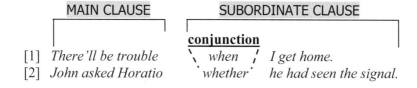

The subordinate clause in [1] is adverbial, and like most time adverbials (here replaceable by the adverb *tomorrow*) can be moved to the front of the sentence or be dispensed with. Not so the subordinate clause in [2], which is a noun clause (replaceable by the noun *something*), the second of two objects required by the verb *ask*.

Observe a subordinate clause in a tree diagram:

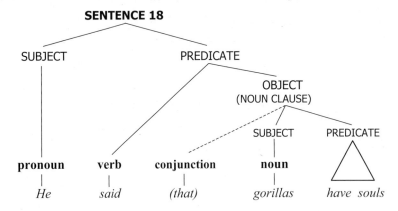

Not all subordinate clauses look as neat as the one above – many have 'invisible' subjects and/or objects, which can be shown 'resurfaced' on the board if such clarification is required.

The list of clause types below is not exhaustive but reasonably complete for ELT purposes. All are adverbial except for those marked. Those requiring fuller treatment are dealt with in later chapters.

16.4 Subordinate clauses

Task 16.1 Four of the rows below are mismatched. Match them correctly (columns 2 and 3 remain intact).

TYPE	EXAMPLE	SUBORDINATING CONJUNCTION
1. conditional	a) ***If I sang out of tune*** *you would walk out on me.*	*if, unless, as long as, supposing*
2. contrast	b) ***Although I had a map*** *I still managed to get lost.*	*although, though, despite the fact that*
3. gerund (noun clause)	c) ***Cutting out coupons*** *is her hobby.*	Ø
4. -ing participle – reason	d) ***Knowing the lie of the land,*** *Glenn volunteered for the patrol.*	Ø
5. -ing participle – time	e) ***Driven by a desire to win,*** *Ellen clung to the helm.*	Ø
6. manner/ comparative	f) *She sang **as she had never sung before**.*	*as, as if/though, like, than*
7. past participle	g) ***Stepping onto the moon,*** *Neil began to utter the famous words.*	Ø
8. purpose	h) *I put up a fence **so as not to be disturbed by the passing yobs**.*	*to, in order to, so, so that, so as to*
9. relative (postmodifying clause)	i) *The hand **that rocks the cradle** rules the world.*	*who, that, which, whose, where, when*
10. reported speech (noun clause)	j) *They said **(that) they wanted peace**.*	*(that), if, whether*
11. time	k) *Well, **since you didn't even send her a Valentine card** I'm not convinced.*	*because, since, as*
12. reason	l) *I haven't seen him **since he blew three grand at Epsom**.*	*since, when, before, after, while, as, until*

Improving customer service

Recommended ways of improving customer service include:

1 __*returning*__ calls promptly.

2 _____ key customers special discounts.

3 _____ research to find out what customers need.

4 _____ staff training programmes in customer care.

5 _____ procedures so they are customer-focussed.

6 _____ clear performance targets.

7 _____ results in order to review progress.

From *Market Leader Upper Intermediate* by D. Cotton et al (Longman). Gerund clauses.

16.4.1 Perfect -ing participle clause

> *Having burnt his bridges*, *Lee had no choice but to go on.*

These non-finite clauses have the time reference 'previous to the main clause', and as with 4 and 5 in task 16.1 above indicate reason or time, but more often the former.

16.5 Correlative coordination

Correlative coordinators/conjunctions are pairs of words or phrases connecting words, phrases or sentences. They consist of *both ... and, (n)either ... (n)or, not only ... but also,* etc.:

> *Neither a borrower **nor** a lender be.*
> *They **not only** pulled the plug, **(but)** they **(also)** ripped out the sink.*

Broad negative adverbs (9.2.5) also act as correlative coordinators with *when*:

> *The words had **hardly** left my mouth **when** the roof caved in.*

Remember that inversion (see 9.2.5) comes into play when the negative adverbial is fronted:

> ***Not only** did they pull the plug, **(but)** they **(also)** ripped out the sink.*
> ***Hardly** had the words left my mouth **when** the roof caved in.*

---

1 Join the two halves of the famous quotes. The first one has been done for you.

1	Time is like a river made up of events. No sooner does anything appear	a)	to such great account.
2	Not until it is too late	b)	do I have the true feeling of myself.
3	Only when I am unbearably unhappy	c)	does one recognise the really important moments in one's life.
4	Not only should justice be done,	d)	to do so much.
5	Never before have we had so little time	e)	than it is swept away and something else comes into its place.
6	Not only is the universe queerer than we suppose,	f)	but it should manifestly and undoubtedly be seen do be done.
7	Never has a man turned so little knowledge	g)	he did not suffer them at all.
8	Not only did he not suffer fools gladly,	h)	but queerer than we *can* suppose.

2 Match the quotes with the people below. Check your answers on page 134.

a) Roman Emperor Marcus Aurelius Antoninus philosophising about change. *Quote 1*

b) US President Franklin D. Roosevelt in a speech to Congress in 1941.

c) Former Lord Chief Justice of the United Kingdom, Gordon Hewitt.

d) British geneticist J.B.S. Haldane contemplating extraterrestrial life.

e) Anonymous: about US Statesman Dean Gooderham Acheson.

f) Dramatist and poet T.S. Elliot talking about Shakespeare.

g) Crime writer Agatha Christie reflecting on her life.

From *Inside Out Advanced* by C. Jones & T. Bastow (Macmillan Heinemann). Negative adverbials, correlative coordination and inversion.

17 Reported speech

17.1 Definition

In reported speech (also called *indirect speech*) we report what was said. The most common verbs used for this are *say, tell, ask, explain,* even *think,* etc, and ones met at higher levels would include *suggest, hint, boast, demand, insist,* etc. (for *suggest/recommend* type verbs see 19.9).

We could repeat the speaker's words (direct speech) where these are important, or for drama or immediacy:

> *He said, "Let's get the hell out of here!"*

But normally we use reported speech, and this allows us to colour the utterance somewhat:

> *He said it might be a good idea to vacate the premises.*

However, there are structure rules which generally apply.

17.2 Reported statements – back shift

In reported statements the subordinate clause following the reporting verb has the form of a noun clause. We can call this subordinate clause a reported speech clause.

A typical rule covered by coursebooks is: "When the reporting verb in the main clause is in the past tense, **back-shift** occurs, i.e. the verb in the reported speech clause changes from present to past, present perfect to past perfect, or past to past perfect as the case requires." But of course this rule need not always apply:

DIRECT STATEMENT	REPORTED STATEMENT
[1] *"I'll be there at eight."*	She said (that) she'd/she'll be here at eight.
[2] *"I've seen better."*	She remarked that she had/has seen better.
[3] *"I saw Nessie last year."*	He told me (that) he had seen/saw the monster the previous year.

In [1], if the time of the reporting is still before eight o'clock, *She said she'll be here* is equally acceptable, though *would* can be used to imply some mistrust. After eight, however, only *would* is acceptable. [2] is similarly flexible. In [3] the past simple is an alternative where ambiguity would not arise .

17.3 Reported questions

In forming most direct questions subject-operator inversion occurs in the subordinate clause, i.e. the (first) auxiliary verb or *be* is moved from post-subject to pre-subject position. When the question is reported, however, affirmative word order is restored.

17.3.1 Reported wh- questions

DIRECT WH- QUESTION	REPORTED WH- QUESTION
"Where have all the flowers gone?"	She wants to know where all the flowers have gone.
"Where have all the flowers gone?"	She asked me/wondered/wanted to know where all the flowers had gone.

There is a growing tendency to accept the direct question form in spoken reported questions, especially in the case of short questions with the verb *be*. However, it may not be wise to teach these as yet:

> *She asked me what size was the shirt.* ~ *She asked me what size the shirt was.*

17.3.2 Reported yes/no questions

To report a yes/no question, *if* or *whether* is used. *Whether* seems preferable when there is more of an aspect of choice. *Or not* may be inserted immediately after *whether* or at the end of the clause beginning with *if* or *whether*. It conveys a 'make up your mind' tone.

DIRECT YES/NO QUESTION	REPORTED YES/NO QUESTION
?	I was wondering whether (or not)° you would take the bait (or not)°.
"Are you hanging up your stockings?"	She asked (me) if I was hanging up my stockings (or not).

The 'choice' property of *whether* is revealed in other contexts:

> *Whether it sells or not is up to the market.*
> *I didn't know whether to laugh or cry.*

17.4 Reported commands, advice, requests

Reported commands, advice, requests, etc, generally use the infinitive. There is often difficulty in forming the negative infinitive:

DIRECT COMMAND	REPORTED COMMAND
"Play the piano."	She ordered/told/advised/persuaded/asked us to play the piano.
"Don't play the sax."	She " " " " not to play the sax.

Teaching note 17.1

The caveat of not overdoing grammatical transformations is worth reiterating here. Exercises where students are asked to change a text or a list of sentences from one grammatical form to another (e.g. from direct to reported speech and vice versa) are rarely seen now, thankfully.

If practice is to be given it is better designed for the role of a news reporter etc. Apart from this, most direct and reported speech is better left as is; after all, when we read *She said she didn't support it*, do we automatically think: *She said, "I don't support it"*?

17.5 'Be like' as reporting verb

There is a tendency among younger speakers to use especially *was like* instead of *said* or describing a reaction in more specific terms, e.g.

> *She just stared at me and I was like, "Hello, have you got a problem?"*

It remains to be seen if this colloquial novelty becomes acceptable in standard English.

17.6 *Say* and *tell*

He said me... is a common error. *Say* doesn't take a personal object. *He said to me* is a typical correction but this is more usual for emphasis or in a question, e.g. *What did he say to you?* Therefore, *he told me,* or simply *he said,* would perhaps be a better correction.

Say conveys any utterance, *tell* only conveys information or instruction. *Tell* is often di-transitive, i.e. it takes two objects, the person told and the information told. Exceptions are *tell the time, tell a lie,* etc.

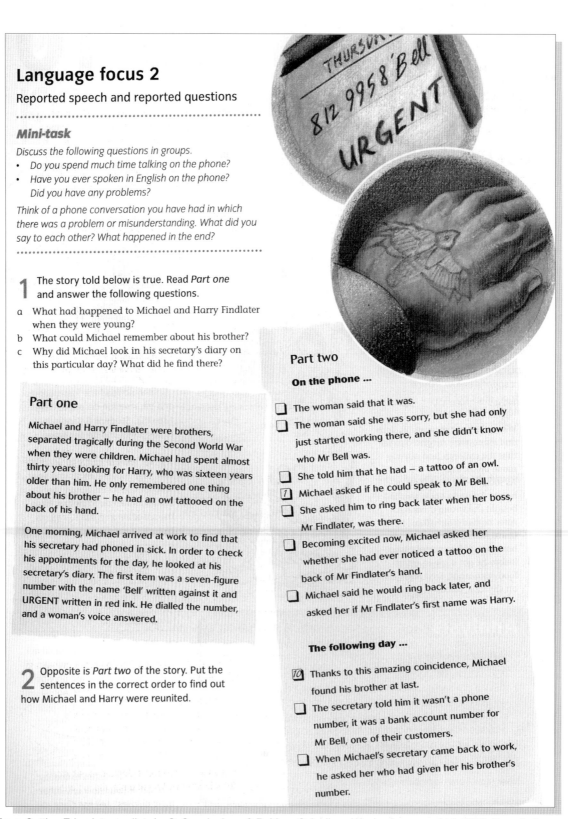

Language focus 2

Reported speech and reported questions

··

Mini-task

Discuss the following questions in groups.
- *Do you spend much time talking on the phone?*
- *Have you ever spoken in English on the phone?*
  Did you have any problems?

Think of a phone conversation you have had in which there was a problem or misunderstanding. What did you say to each other? What happened in the end?

··

1 The story told below is true. Read *Part one* and answer the following questions.

a   What had happened to Michael and Harry Findlater when they were young?

b   What could Michael remember about his brother?

c   Why did Michael look in his secretary's diary on this particular day? What did he find there?

Part one

Michael and Harry Findlater were brothers, separated tragically during the Second World War when they were children. Michael had spent almost thirty years looking for Harry, who was sixteen years older than him. He only remembered one thing about his brother – he had an owl tattooed on the back of his hand.

One morning, Michael arrived at work to find that his secretary had phoned in sick. In order to check his appointments for the day, he looked at his secretary's diary. The first item was a seven-figure number with the name 'Bell' written against it and URGENT written in red ink. He dialled the number, and a woman's voice answered.

2 Opposite is *Part two* of the story. Put the sentences in the correct order to find out how Michael and Harry were reunited.

Part two

On the phone ...

☐ The woman said that it was.

☐ The woman said she was sorry, but she had only just started working there, and she didn't know who Mr Bell was.

☐ She told him that he had – a tattoo of an owl.

☐ **1** Michael asked if he could speak to Mr Bell.

☐ She asked him to ring back later when her boss, Mr Findlater, was there.

☐ Becoming excited now, Michael asked her whether she had ever noticed a tattoo on the back of Mr Findlater's hand.

☐ Michael said he would ring back later, and asked her if Mr Findlater's first name was Harry.

The following day ...

☐ **10** Thanks to this amazing coincidence, Michael found his brother at last.

☐ The secretary told him it wasn't a phone number, it was a bank account number for Mr Bell, one of their customers.

☐ When Michael's secretary came back to work, he asked her who had given her his brother's number.

From *Cutting Edge Intermediate* by S. Cunningham & P. Moor © Addison Wesley Longman Ltd. 1999. Reported speech.

18 Relative clauses

18.1 Types; terminology

There are mainly two types of relative clause, **identifying** and **non-identifying**. Some grammars use the term *defining* or *restrictive* instead of *identifying*.

In this chapter we also look at reduced relative clauses and cleft sentences.

18.2 Identifying relative clauses

We can put an adjective before a noun to modify/identify it, e.g. *The **early** boat carries the mail.* We may also post-modify the noun, usually with a relative clause, e.g. *The boat **that leaves early** carries the mail.* This modification is necessary to identify the boat that the speaker mentions, and this type of clause is called an **identifying** relative clause. Become acquainted with the rules governing choice of relative pronoun by carrying out the task below.

THINGS	1. *The piano **that went for fifty quid** has woodworm.* 2. *The piano **which was owned by Chopin** is not on display.*	....
	3. *The boat **whose sails are ripped** will be last.*	....
	4. *The boat **I saw** didn't have rowlocks.*	....
	5. *That's the tower **where Strongbow married Aoife.***	....
PEOPLE	6. *The woman **who refused to give up her seat** was brave.* 7. *There's the hunk **that lit your fire.***	....
	8. *The woman **whose son is a lexicographer** would like a word.*	....
	9. *The chiropodist **you hired** hasn't put a foot wrong.*	....

Task 18.1 Put the letters of the rules below into the correct cells in the right hand column of the table above. Some letters will go in more than one cell.

a) The relative pronoun *that* or *which* can refer back to things (*which* sounds more formal).
b) The relative pronoun *who* or *that* can refer back to people (*that* sounds a little less respectful).
c) The possessive relative determiner can refer back to people or things.
d) The relative adverbs *where* and *when* are often preferred over *in which, on which,* where applicable.
e) If the relative pronoun is the object of the verb in the relative clause (although it goes before it) then it can be deleted.

5 The definitions in column A are ungrammatical. Correct each one by ~~crossing out~~ one unnecessary word. Then match the definitions with a word from column B.

A
a) An animal that ~~it~~ can smell water five kilometres away.
b) A person who he studies birds.
c) An animal that it sleeps standing up.
d) The only animal – apart from humans – which it gets sunburn.
e) A name for people who they are afraid of spiders.
f) The thing that you sit on it when you ride a horse.
g) An insect that you get malaria from it.
h) An animal whose name it means 'I don't understand.'

B
1 A saddle.
2 A kangaroo.
3 A mosquito.
4 An elephant.
5 An ornithologist.
6 A pig.
7 A horse.
8 Arachnophobic.

6 Use the ideas in the boxes (and your own) to write down three true statements about your feelings or the feelings of people you know well. Compare your statements with a partner.

| I My mother My father My friend etc. | + | love(s) hate(s) | + | people men women children animals bars shops rooms etc. | + | who which that | + | are funny / serious. talk too quietly / loudly. are very cheap / expensive. drive too slowly / fast. are very big / small etc. |

From *Inside Out Pre-intermediate* by S. Kay et al (Macmillan). Identifying relative clauses.

18.3 Non-identifying relative clause

18.3.1 With the antecedent being a noun/phrase

Unlike identifying relative clauses, non-identifying relative clauses are not essential for an understanding of the sentence, as the antecedent in the main clause needs no identifying – it is either [1] a proper noun (name of a person, place, institution, etc.), [2] known to the interlocuters, or [3] already identified in some way:

[1] *Roberto Calvi, **who was known as 'God's banker',** was found hanged in London.*
[2] *... and then someone stole his bike, **which he'd only bought the week before**.*
[3] *It establishes a Union, **within which the policies of the Member States shall be ...***

Task 18.2 Fill in the blanks:

A non-identifying relative clause is set off from the (a) _____ clause by a comma/commas; in speech, a pause and change in (b) _____ are used. Compare with identifying relative clauses.

The relative pronoun (c) '_____' is not used in non-identifying clauses.

In either type of relative clause the object form of *who* must be used after a preposition, e.g. *the man with* (d) _____ *she was living.*

18.3.2 With the antecedent being the main clause

In this case there is only one pronoun used: *which.*

[1] *He offered me some peanuts, **which was very strange** (as he didn't have any).*
[2] *Anne described the projector bulb, **which shed some light on the matter**.*

Sentence [2] can be ambiguous. The intended meaning is that it was Anne's description of the bulb that shed light on the matter, not the bulb itself. However, the use in English of identical relative pronouns for different types of relative clause gives rise to sometimes comical interpretations.

4 Work with a partner. Look at each of the following sentence pairs and decide which is the most suitable follow-up sentence (1 or 2).

Main sentence	Follow-up sentence
a) She offered me some cigarettes that were very strange. b) She offered me some cigarettes, which was very strange.	1 They were red and blue. 2 She knows I don't smoke.
c) He's going out with Julie, who I can't stand. d) He's going out with Julie, which I can't stand.	1 He should be going out with me! 2 She's such a gossip.
e) She bought me an expensive tie which I didn't like. f) She bought me an expensive tie, which I didn't like.	1 Why waste money on ties? 2 It was a horrible orange colour.
g) My brother who lives in Rome is a model. h) My brother, who lives in Rome, is a model.	1 My other brother is an accountant. 2 He absolutely loves his job.

From *Inside Out Upper Intermediate* by S. Kay & V. Jones (Macmillan). Identifying and non-identifying relative clauses.

Task 18.3 Do the exercise from *Inside Out Upper Intermediate* above.

18.4 Reduced relative clause

A reduced relative clause uses a participle, dropping the relative pronoun and *be:*

>They watched the motor cars (which were) **racing** through the town.
>They watched the motor cars (which were being) **driven** by men with funny helmets.

This structure is preferred for a more formal register. The -ing participle is active, the past participle is passive. Understood elements may also include modals.

Note that these participle clauses are post-modifying and restrictive, unlike the ones in 16.4 which are non-restrictive and usually adverbial (of reason, time). Further analysis is not merited, but do remember that the subject of a participle clause must be the same as that of its main clause, otherwise we have what is called a 'dangling participle', e.g *?Watching the motor cars, a loose wheel killed one of the spectators* is not generally acceptable.

Task 18.4 Identify the subordinate clauses below (reduced relatives, participle and reported speech):

The man identified as the main suspect was spotted downtown last weekend. The head of the detective unit, speaking on television last night, warned that the man was dangerous and anyone seeing him should keep their distance.

18.5 Cleft sentences

[1a] *It was curds and whey (that) Miss Moffat ate.*
[1b] *It was Miss Moffat that/who ate the curds and whey.*
[1c] **It was eat the curds and whey that Miss Moffat did.*
[2a] *What Miss Moffat ate was curds and whey.*
[2b] **Who ate the curds and whey was Miss Moffat.*
[2c] *What she did was (to) eat the curds and whey.*

Cleft sentences are not relative clauses as we know them but are often presented soon after them.

In a cleft sentence a particular element is highlighted. *It* cleft sentences [1] start with *It* + *be* and follow with the highlighted element moved out of its normal position. *Wh-* cleft sentences [2] contain a *wh-* noun clause, usually in initial position.

There are some restrictions, two shown above: [1c] demonstrates how *it* + *be* is not acceptable before a finite verb, and [2b] demonstrates how a *who-* (as subject) clause is not usually acceptable.

Use of English: open cloze
(Part 2)

1 Discuss these questions.

1 How many people in the class have a bottle of water with them now?
2 Why do people buy bottled water?

2 Read the title and the text below to get a general idea of what it is about. How does it answer question 2 above?

DESIGNER WATER
– The New Accessory

Many tourists nowadays walk around carrying plastic bottles (0) ...*of*.... water, even in cities. The bottles seem to (1) .... become an important fashion accessory, and not (2) .... for tourists. In fact, nowadays everyone seems to carry a bottle of water with (3) .... wherever they go. This fashion for being seen with bottled water, sometimes called 'designer water', (4) .... led to a massive increase (5) .... sales over the past few years. There are now (6) .... many different brand names available in the shops that it is hard to choose.

But (7) .... do some people prefer their water from a bottle rather than a tap? To start with, water forms (8) .... vital part of a healthy lifestyle. We (9) .... now advised to drink two litres of water daily, as (10) .... as eating large quantities of fruit and vegetables. In addition (11) .... this, designer water offers the promise of purity. (12) .... is advertised as clean and natural, while tap water may be viewed (13) .... suspicion.

But is there really any difference (14) .... bottled and tap water? Surprisingly, in (15) .... USA it was found that bottled water was not always as pure as most ordinary tap water.

3 You have to complete the spaces in the text with one word. The words are usually grammatical. First, look at the following sets of words and match them with the grammatical labels a)–h) below.

Example: *Group 1 are all expressions of quantity.*

1 *any few little many no some*
2 *a an one the*
3 *it them they you*
4 *what where which who why*
5 *as less more than*
6 *anyone anything everything everywhere whatever whoever*
7 *am is are was were has have had being having*
8 *at for from in with of on to with*

a) articles/numbers
b) auxiliary verbs
c) comparatives
d) expressions of quantity
e) indefinite pronouns
f) personal pronouns
g) prepositions
h) relative pronouns/question words

TIP! You will find it easier to do this task if you think about what type of word is missing.

4 Read the text again and think of the word which best fits each space. Use only one word in each space. There is an example at the beginning (0). You will find most of the words you need in Exercise 3.

From *New First Certificate Gold* by J. Newbrook et al © Pearson Education Ltd 2004. Cloze passage, various items including relative pronouns.

Task 18.5   Do the matching task (right column) from *New First Certificate Gold* above.

19 Conditionals

19.1 Definition

Although we have referred to conditional *clauses* in chapter 16, the term *conditional* usually refers to any *sentence* with an *if* clause and a main or result clause.

In TESOL three types of conditional are given prominence. As well as these the coursebooks may also present the 'zero' conditional so this is included in our table below. Mixed conditionals are shown later.

19.2 Table of the three conditionals, with the zero conditional

	IF CLAUSE	RESULT (MAIN) CLAUSE
Zero conditional	PRESENT (/PAST) TENSE *If (= when(ever)) we* **have** *the money* FUNCTION: fact, circumstance, logic	PRESENT (/PAST) TENSE *we* **go** *to the movies.*
1st conditional	PRESENT TENSE *If he* **studies** *this book* FUNCTION: future probable	FUTURE *he* **will** *pass.*
2nd conditional	PAST TENSE *If you* **smoked** *less* FUNCTION: unreal for the present/future	WOULD *you* **would** *feel better.*
3rd conditional	PAST PERFECT TENSE *If I* **had known** *you were coming* FUNCTION: unreal for the past	WOULD HAVE *I* **would have** *baked a cake.*

Please note that of course these are not all taught at the same level; the common timing in the ELT coursebooks is pre-intermediate, intermediate and upper intermediate for 1st, 2nd and 3rd conditional respectively (the zero conditional may be acquired without any direct teaching). See the appendix for a view of all levels with their grammatical items.

19.3 The zero conditional

Besides the present tense (see table above) a past tense may also be contained in a zero conditional, conveying a fact, logical conclusion, etc.:

[1] *If (= when(ever)) we had the money we went to the movies.*
[2] *Well, if he was there I didn't see him.*
[3] *It cuts out if (= when(ever)) you put your foot to the floor.*
[4] *If it's Tuesday it must be Paris.*
[5] *If you are married you don't have to do military service.*

Students rarely have difficulty in acquiring the zero conditional, so please respect the dictum: IF THEY KNOW IT, DON'T TEACH IT. That being said, *if* is translatable into German as 'wenn', resulting in errors like ?*When you are married you don't have to do military service.* Be prepared to explain, with examples of course, that *when* means a time, often an expected time of completion, whereas *if* conveys conditionality.

19.4 1st Conditional

	IF CLAUSE	RESULT (MAIN) CLAUSE
1st Conditional	PRESENT TENSE *If he **studies** this book* FUNCTION: future probable	FUTURE *he **will** pass.*

The verb in the *if* clause is in the present tense (usually simple, but continuous and perfect are also possible), the verb in the result clause is in the future tense. This future 'tense' of course can have many forms besides the usual *will*, e.g. the modal *might/could* etc, indeed *going to* or present continuous where suitable, e.g. *If it rains we're going (to go) to the cinema.*:

[1] *If you **study** this book, you **will** have a good grounding in grammar.*
[2] *We'll/we **might** go to the cinema if it **rains**.*
[3] *If it **should** (happen to) **rain**, we'll go to the cinema.*
[4] *If you **see** Nora, **give** her this note.*

Task 19.1   Fill in the blanks. The numbers refer to the examples above.

> 1-3. The 1st conditional is often given the functional/time title (a) *f_____ conditional*. It could also be called the *quite probable conditional*. In any event these terms should only be used when required, for example when comparing 1st and 2nd conditionals, which is not a communicatively valuable exercise but may be requested for exam preparation.
>
> 1.   A common error is **If you* (b) _____ *study this book*. You should point out that English does not use a future tense in a subordinate *if* or time clause, or as a student might put it: "no *will* after *if* or *when*." There is an exception: *If you will please take your seats ...* , used for a request, deferring ostensibly to the *willingness* of the listeners – but to avoid confusion don't introduce this till later.
>
> 2.   Regarding punctuation, the (c) _____ is optional when the (d) _____ clause comes first. The other way round it would signal an afterthought.
>
> 3.   *Should* and/or *happen to* is sometimes inserted in the *if* clause to convey that the probability of the occurrence is (e) sl_____. *Should* may begin the sentence when a more formal (f) r_____ is required, e.g. *Should it (happen to) rain ...* .
>
> 4.   The (g) im_____ in the main clause is a 'hidden' future, so this is a 1st conditional.

Unless roughly means *except if,* usually occurring in 1st or 2nd conditional structures.

Phrases like *supposing/provided that, as long as, imagine,* etc, can also trigger conditional structures.

Teaching note 19.1

Coursebooks commonly teach the first conditional with the situation of someone embarking on a journey/activity that their friend/mother thinks is risky, e.g. the couple moving to Spain (New Headway Intermediate) or the son going hitch-hiking (New Cambridge English 1). The dialogue typically goes:
A: *We're moving to Italy.*
B: *Are you sure you're doing the right thing? What will you do if you can't find a good home/if you don't make any friends?* [etc.]
A: *Don't worry. If we don't ... we'll ...*

Future time clauses with *when, as soon as*, etc, may be introduced:
B: *How will I know you're okay?*
A: *Don't worry, Mum. I'll text you as soon as I arrive ...*

Dialogues/role plays allow students to have fun while improving their speaking skills. Try to add to/extend the ones in your coursebook.

19.5 2nd Conditional

	IF CLAUSE	RESULT (MAIN) CLAUSE
2nd Conditional	PAST TENSE *If you **smoked** less*	*WOULD* *you **would** feel better.*
	FUNCTION: unreal for the present/future	

Also called the 'unreal' or 'contrary to fact' conditional, the 2nd conditional is a little difficult to acquire because of its peculiar use of the past tense for a hypothetical event.

The verb in the *if* clause is in the past tense form, the verb in the result clause is preceded by the modal *would* or *could*, or *might*:

> [1] *If I **had** a million dollars **I'd** buy a helicopter.*
> [2] *What **would** you do if you **won** the lottery?*
> [3] *If I **were** you, I **would** recommend this book to my friends.*
> [4] *If Elvis **were/was** alive, he'**d** gyrate in his grave.*
> [5] ***Had** I their support I **could** change the leadership overnight.*
> [6] *John, if you **could/would** turn on the light there, please.*

Task 19.2 Fill in the blanks. The numbers refer to the examples above.

1. This is a typical example of the use of the 2nd conditional for situations (in the *if* clause) which, for most people, are (a) _____ [some options available here].

2. This is a typical example of the use of the 2nd conditional for highly (b) im_____ events (in the *if* clause).

3. Instead of *was* after the 1st (c) _____ singular, *were* is widely preferred. This *were* is a relic of the (d) sub_____ mood, used in many languages to denote unreal events. Note also that in BrE (e) _____ is sometimes used instead of *would* in this type of sentence (subject pronoun in 1st person in main clause).

4. With the 3rd person singular there is a freer choice concerning *were* or *was*; however, (f) _____ is still more colloquial than (g) _____ .

5. For a more formal register, *had* may be inverted with the subject (the *if* being omitted). This is also possible, though less frequently done, with another verb in the list, which is (h) _____ .

6. This 'unfinished' 2nd conditional is a very popular form of polite (i) r_____ , though rarely included in coursebooks! *Could/would* may be regarded as the past of *can/will* here.

Teaching note 19.2

Make sure your examples of the 2nd conditional refer to unreal or highly improbable events. "What <u>would</u> you do if you <u>won</u> the lottery?" is fine, but in many contexts so is "What <u>will</u> you do if you <u>win</u> the raffle?" (1st conditional for probable events).

Check if your students understand the word *imagine* or even *hypothesis;* this often helps to explain the function of the 2nd conditional (a brief translation of a model sentence may also help).

Practice activities may sometimes fall flat if you don't put a little imagination into them. For example, the lead-in question "What would you do if you won the lottery?" may get some yawns – travel around the world, buy a Ferrari ... – but with a little stimulation the activity might become more lively. Remind students that with a generous charitable donation their name might live on for a long time, or if they were to throw the most magnificent party ever in their town, imagine, you could invite your favourite celebrity or world leader to sit at your table, in fact you could probably change the world, at least your town, for the better.

If the teacher-fronted activity is not drawing much participation then a) you're not allowing enough time for students to compose and present their answer – don't be afraid of silence; b) there could be some anxiety about giving a display answer – change to pairwork, putting topics/questions on the board.

Coursebooks and resource books usually have good presentation (reading/listening texts) and practice activities. After some time you will remember which topics/activities work best and be able to extend the coursebook ones, e.g. you might prepare cards with questions such as *If someone gave you a gift voucher worth €300 for a DIY store what would you buy?* Change the amount and the store, or the situation (wedding/birthday) and the requirement (what to wear) and you've got many other cards. Use the cards in a typical group/pair activity: cards face down, a student picks one up, reads and answers or asks another student to answer, others comment, and so on. Don't forget that students can be invited to write some of these cards – they can be very imaginative.

Teaching note 19.3

CARDS FOR 2ND CONDITIONAL PRACTICE:
(students must try to say at least three things in their answer)

If someone gave you a gift voucher worth €300 for a DIY store what would you buy?	If someone gave you a gift voucher worth €200 for a music store/website what would you buy?
If there was a power cut in this building what would happen?	If someone invited you to a fancy dress party what would you wear?
If you had to raise €3,000 for a local charity what would you do?	If you were asked to organise a stag/hen party for your friend what would you do?
If you were alone on a desert island what would you do?	If you were blind what would you be doing now?
If you had to cook a meal for your boss/teacher what would you cook?	If you had to go to hospital for two months what would you take with you?

19.6 3rd Conditional

	IF CLAUSE	RESULT (MAIN) CLAUSE
3rd Conditional	PAST PERFECT TENSE *If I had known you were coming* FUNCTION: unreal for the past	*WOULD HAVE* *I would have baked a cake.*

Functionally, this is the 'what might have been' conditional, commonly called the *past conditional*.

Both clauses refer to past time. The verb in the *if* clause is in the past perfect tense, the verb in the result clause is preceded by *would have* (or *could/might have*, rarely *should have*):

[1] *If I **had known** you were coming, I **would have** baked a cake.*
[2] ***Had I known** you were coming, I **would have** baked a cake.*
[3] ***Had I had** notice of your coming, I **would have** baked a cake.*
[4] *If Napoleon **had had** more patience, he **wouldn't have** suffered at Waterloo.*

Task 19.3   Fill in the blanks. The numbers refer to the examples above.

1. The (a) _____ forms *If I'd known ... I would've ...* shouldn't be withheld from the learners as this is how these phrases are normally spoken.

2,3. As in the 2nd conditional, the subject and *had* may be inverted (the *if* being omitted), but in this case the first *had* is not the main verb but the (b) _____ verb.

4. For presentation and practice, (c) _____ examples are always better than made-up ones. Don't forget recent events in the learners' environment. And <u>don't</u> present *had had* or inverted forms until learners are comfortable with the basic forms.

1 Complete sentence b) in each pair so that it has a similar meaning to sentence a).

1 a) It's likely there is life on other planets. If so, we are not alone.
 b) If there .... life on other planets, we .... not alone.
2 a) The world's population will probably continue to increase. If so, we will need more food.
 b) If the world's population .... to increase, we .... more food.
3 a) Other intelligent beings might inhabit the universe. If so, they would be very different from us.
 b) If other intelligent beings .... the universe, they .... very different from us.
4 a) There aren't many TV programmes about science, so people don't know much about it.
 b) If there .... more TV programmes about science, people .... more about it.
5 a) We shouldn't have spent so much money on space research. Instead, we could have solved many other serious problems.
 b) If we .... less on space research, we .... many other serious problems.

2   There is a mistake with the verb in the second part of each sentence. Correct the mistakes so the second part follows on correctly from the first part.

1 He will pass his driving test if he will practise.
2 You can borrow the car tonight if you would take good care of it.
3 I wouldn't have made so much food if I knew they weren't coming.
4 If you buy two, you got a third one free.
5 I would have done better if I worked harder.
6 If I had the right tools, I can fix the flat tyre myself.
7 If you'd told me Susan was going to be there, I would never go to the party.
8 If I lived in that house, I will get smoke alarms put in straightaway.

From *New First Certificate Gold* by J. Newbrook et al © Pearson Education Ltd 2004. Conditionals

> **Task 19.4**   Do exercise 1 in the extract above, then identify the type of conditional each sentence is. The first one has been done for you here:
>
> 1b) *If there is life on other planets, we are not alone. ZERO CONDITIONAL.*

19.7 Mixed conditionals

When a sentence has one clause showing a 3rd conditional structure and a second one showing a 2nd conditional structure this sentence is said to contain 'mixed conditionals'.

The *if* clause may refer to a past time (3rd cond.) and the result clause to the present time (2nd cond.):

> *If I **had taken** his advice I **would**n't be in this mess now.*

Less commonly, the order may be reversed, i.e. the if clause may refer to the present time (2nd conditional) and the result clause to a past time (3rd conditional):

> *If he **wanted** to go he **would have** booked it before now.*

19.8 The hypothetical past / past subjunctive

The *were* in *If I **were** you* is said to be a relic of the **past subjunctive** in English, and for all other verbs in similar structures the **hypothetical past** is used, e.g. *If I **won** a million quid; If only I **had** a million quid; I wish you **didn't/wouldn't** smoke so much (would* is the past of *will* here*); It's time we **went** home; As if I **cared**.*

This hypothetical past is sometimes also called the past subjunctive; this would require the invention of 'past perfect subjunctive' for 3rd conditional and *I wish I **hadn't smoked** beforehand,* etc, but such argument is not for here.

19.9 The present subjunctive

The **present subjunctive** has the form of the bare infinitive and is used in *that-* clauses after 'suggest/recommend' type verbs. There is an optional *should*:

> *The board recommends/ed that the accounts (should) **be** checked.*
> *She insists/ed that I (should) **call** the cops.*

Another option after the past form, e.g. *recommended/insisted* above, is *were* and *called,* e.g.

> *The board recommended that the accounts **were** checked.*
> *She insisted that I **called** the cops.*

but the potential ambiguity of the past tense in the subordinate clause (is it real or hypothetical?) makes the present subjunctive a better choice.

The present subjunctive is also to be found in some formulaic expressions:

> ***Be** that as it may; **Suffice** (it) to say,* etc.

19.10 American English

Many AmE speakers use *would (have)* in the *if* clauses in the 2nd and 3rd conditional:

> *If I **would know** her address, I **would** visit her now.*
> (instead of *If I **knew** her address…)*
> *If you **would have** persisted, you **would have** gotten through*
> (instead of *If you **had** persisted…).*

This usage may become globally acceptable in time. For the moment, however, it is advisable to present only the orthodox pattern.

19.11 *I wish* and *if only*

These phrases are often presented in coursebooks at late intermediate and upper intermediate levels. They operate similarly to *if* in 2nd and 3rd conditionals, although the *I wish* clause does not follow with a result clause, whereas *if only* may or may not.

I wish is often used as a follow-on (see the extract on the right) or an introduction to a topic. It is also used for expressing regret *(I wish I could help you but ...)* especially before a refusal.

If only is more emphatic and can imply less personal involvement and a more precise or obvious benefit:

unreal present:

> *I wish (/if only) I had a million quid.*
> *If we only had the weather.*

unreal past:

> *I wish (/if only) I had invested in mobile phones.*
> *If only he had listened.*

1 Read Cris's story. Then match each sentence 1–8 to one of his wishes a)–h) below.

1 I think I'm in love with Eleanor. *h)*
2 She's going out with Carlo.
3 He's the captain of the basketball team.
4 He's very rich and he drives a silver BMW.
5 Eleanor's eyes light up when she sees him driving it.
6 I heard there was a big party yesterday for the basketball team and Eleanor was there.
7 They say Carlo drove another girl home from the party and Eleanor was crying.
8 But I know she'll never leave Carlo, even though he'll never make her happy.

a) I wish she would look at **me** like that.
b) I wish I'd been invited.
c) I wish I'd had a clean tissue to dry her tears.
d) I wish I had lots of money and a big car.
e) I wish she was going out with me instead.
f) I wish I could get picked for the team too.
g) I wish she'd never met him. I could make her much happier.
h) I wish I wasn't – I don't have a chance with her.

From *New First Certificate Gold* by J. Newbrook et al.
© Pearson Education Ltd 2004. *Wish* + hypothetical past.

19.12 Conditional 'tense'

Some grammars categorize clauses containing *would* as having a conditional 'tense'. To avoid confusion it would be better to confine *conditional* to sentences and call *would* simply *would*.

Of course there is some justification for the word 'conditional' when explaining the use of , e.g. *Emma **would**n't do that* (on any condition) or *I'd say it's fake* (if you asked me). Some grammars use the term 'conditional verb <u>form</u>' or '*would* for hypothetical meaning' for these instances.

19.13 Native speaker errors

For many speakers, in colloquial use there is an inserted *a* in the 3rd conditional:

> *If (only) you had-a stuck at the piano lessons ...*

which may be analogous with the *a* (or *of*) substituted for *have* in the modal perfect:

> *I could-a strangled him.*   *I didn't strangle him but I could of.*

Task 19.5 This is strictly for grammar buffs! Each participant has one or two cards and finds their match. If you are working alone still cut out the cells and match them up.

✂

1. If this clause had a past perfect tense …	it was because the zero conditional was obvious. a)
2. If this clause had had a past simple tense …	we wouldn't be having so much trouble with this 'combo' 3rd & 2nd conditional. b)
3. Unless you show me the right clause …	it would be able to form the 'if' clause of a 3rd conditional sentence. But we now have a 2nd conditional. c)
4. If I found my partner easily …	we will be here all day looking for this 1st conditional. d)
5. If we hadn't looked at this carefully …	that sentence is usually a zero conditional. e)
6. If this clause were in the present tense …	it could have formed the 'if' clause of a 2nd conditional sentence. But now the sentence is a 3rd conditional. f)
7. If we had studied the conditionals more …	it would be able to help form a 1st conditional. Instead we now have a 2nd conditional. g)
8. If I show this to the right person …	we mightn't have formed a 3rd conditional. h)
9. If *whenever* can be substituted for *if* …	they will help me form a 1st conditional. i)

Teaching note 19.4

In case you **still** don't know: this book is not for language learners. Tasks such as the above and lessons which have a purely grammatical content such as a comparison of different types of conditionals don't always hold students' attention. Of course if the students express an interest in or need grammar work in preparation for an exam there is ample justification for it. In which case make sure you are well prepared!

20 The infinitive and -ing form

20.1 Terminology

This chapter looks at various structures involving the infinitive or -ing form.

We have met the infinitive before (1.4, 17.4). In this chapter unless otherwise stated the infinitive is the full infinitive. Also in this chapter, the term **-ing form** is used instead of **gerund** to reflect the terminology of some ELT materials (e.g. *English Grammar in Use* by R. Murphy).

A quick reminder: the gerund can take the place of a noun/-phrase (see 1.11). This includes of course the position of object, which follows most of the main verbs in 20.2 below.

20.2 Verb + infinitive or -ing form

When two verbs come together (without a pause/comma) the second is either an infinitive or an -ing form. Most of the difficulties that students have to contend with regarding choice and meaning are shown below. More examples are contained in course/resource books:

[1] *He enjoys **to go** to the zoo.	He enjoys **going** to the zoo.
[2] They like **to play**.	They like **playing**.
[3] ?Start **to walk**.	Start **walking**.
[4] Are they starting **to play**?	*Are they **starting** playing?
[5] We stopped **to rest**.	We stopped **resting**.
[6] We tried **to push** it.	We tried **pushing** it.
[7] I won't forget **to write**.	I'll never forget **writing** that.

Task 20.1   Fill in the blanks. The numbers refer to the examples above.

> In [1] there is no free choice. The verb *enjoy* may not be followed by the (a) _____ .
>
> In [2] if there is any difference in meaning (and there isn't in AmE) it is that the (b) _____ suggests the activity is tentative or occasional.
>
> In [3] we see that the 'fulfilment' or 'extended' semantic property of the (c) _____ makes it a better prospect for the imperative.
>
> In [4] we see that English prefers not to run an -ing participle and (d) _____ together.
>
> In [5] we see that the verb *stop* can be followed by either an object, here in the form of the (e) _____ or a reason/purpose clause, here in the form of the (f) _____ .
> (All other verbs in this list are followed by an object.)
>
> In [6] we see that after the verb *try,* the (g) _____ indicates 'experiment'.
>
> In [7] we witness a classic case of how the (h) _____ indicates 'future' or 'speculation', whereas the (i) _____ indicates 'fulfilment'.

20.3 Confusion of the infinitive of purpose with *for* + -ing of function

> [1] *I went to the shop **to buy** a comb. ; ?I went to the shop **for buying** a comb.*
> [2] *?A spanner is a tool **to turn** nuts. ; A spanner is a tool **for turning** nuts.*

Most learners seem to include the erroneous form in [1] in their interlanguage. This is hardly surprising, when we hear *Go to the shop <u>for</u> a comb; What did you go to the shop <u>for</u>?* etc.

The simple explanation of the rule will help, but don't forget to follow with meaningful practice:

> **purpose/intention of the person (agent) > INFINITIVE;**
> **function/use of the instrument > -ING FORM.**

(Some overlap is possible of course.)

3   Match the sentence halves and explain the difference in meaning.

1 I'd like to meet her.
   I like meeting her.
   a) on Saturday mornings, because we go shopping together.
   b) at 9.30 tomorrow morning.
2 I stopped to talk to Rose
   I stopped talking to Rose
   a) because I realised I couldn't trust her.
   b) when I bumped into her on the street.
3 I remembered to phone Jack
   I remembered phoning Jack
   a) and he was very pleased.
   b) although I didn't make a note of the exact time.
4 He tried to write his essay in half an hour
   He tried writing his essay in half an hour
   a) but he couldn't do it.
   b) and he got a bad mark for it.
5 I regret to tell you that
   I really regret
   a) encouraging my brother to apply for the job.
   b) your application has been unsuccessful.

4   Rewrite the following sentences using the verbs in brackets in the correct form. Add a preposition where necessary.

Example: We've thought about whether we should move house. *(consider)*
   We've considered moving house.

1 She interrupts me all the time – it's really annoying. *(keep)*
2 She wants to invite all the family to the party. *(insist)*
3 The man claimed he was a government official. *(pretend)*
4 She hoped that he would explain everything to her. *(want)*
5 I think it's great when I don't have to get up early on holiday! *(enjoy/not)*
6 I shouldn't have written the letter. *(regret)*
7 Even though I was late, the examiner allowed me to take the exam. *(let)*
8 I hate being dependent on other people. *(rely)*

From *New First Certificate Gold* by J. Newbrook et al © Pearson Education Ltd 2004. Infinitives and -ing forms.

20.4 Verb + object + infinitive

20.4.1 Infinitive with or without *to*

Observe:

   [1] *She forced me **to cook** the goose.*
   [2] *She made/had me **cook** it.*   (Note: pref. *I was made to cook it.)*
   [3] *She helped me **(to) cook** it.*   (Note: *she assisted me to cook it / in cooking it.)*

In [1] the infinitive with *to* (full infinitive) is required. In [2] the infinitive without *to* (bare infinitive) is required. In [3] there is a free choice. There is no clue here to help students to choose; the deciding factor is collocation alone. Verbs such as *force, make, have* are called **causative verbs**. See also 11.6 and 13.10.1.

Task 20.2

Write FI (full infinitive), BI (bare infinitive) or E (either) after each verb (and object understood) below.

a) permit ____   b) allow ____   c) bid ____   d) get ____

e) have ____   f) let ____   g) assist ____   h) forbid ____

AmE often uses *have* where BrE prefers *get ... to*:

   [4] *I had the mechanic check the brakes ≈ I got the mechanic to check the brakes.*
   [5] *Have the students write emails ≈ Get the students to write emails.*

20.4.2 Bare infinitive or -ing participle

Sentence [6] below uses the infinitive without *to* to convey that the complete action was observed, whereas [7] uses the -ing participle to convey an 'uncompleted' aspect. The 'sense' verbs *see, feel, hear, notice*, etc, often trigger this choice:

   [6] *I saw her **walk** across the street.*
   [7] *I saw her **walking** across the street.*

21 The articles

21.1 Reference

Articles come under the heading Determiner (see 7.2).

The articles (*a/an, the* and *zero*) have 4 areas of reference in English:

1. Specific   2. Unspecific   3. Generic   4. Unique

21.2 Specific reference

Specific here means an actual example of the referent (referent = the thing/person referred to by the word), e.g. in ***A dog*** approached me I am referring to an actual, specific dog (<u>indefinite</u> but specific). When I continue with *I petted **the dog*** I am still referring to a specific dog, this time the **previously mentioned** (<u>definite</u> and specific) dog. Terms marked ^{UF} below are more <u>user-friendly</u> for TESOL.

For plural and uncountable nouns the indefinite specific marker is zero or unstressed *some:*

REFERENCE/USE	SINGULAR (countable)	PLURAL/UNCOUNTABLE
FIRST MENTIONING^{UF} (indefinite specific)	***A dog*** *approached me.*	*She had **(some) hedgehogs** in her garden.* *There was **(some) wine** on the table.*
PREVIOUSLY MENTIONED^{UF} (definite specific)	*I petted **the dog**.*	*She fed **the hedgehogs**.* *She poured **the wine**.*
SHARED EXPERIENCE/ GENERAL KNOWLEDGE/ SITUATION/CONTEXT (definite specific)	*We took **the TV** with us on holiday.* *When we arrived she set **the table**.*	*The people are fine here but **the buses** never come on time.* *Her garden was nice but **the grass** was too long.*

Forward reference can also apply:

*How much is **the doggy** <u>in the window?</u>*

21.3 Unspecific reference

Unspecific means 'any one(s) of that kind':

*My kingdom for **a horse**! ; **A child** could do that. ; I need **(some) hedgehogs** for this scene.*

21.4 Generic reference

This is the term covering reference to a class rather than an actual member(s) of that class. Note the choice of markers for countable, depending on totality of characteristics or typical example, also on register, ranging from formal/academic *the* down to the most common zero (∅) + plural:

COUNT	***The lion*** *is the king of the jungle.* ***The pen*** *is mightier than the sword.*	*A lion can be dangerous.* *A pen can be dangerous.*	*∅ **Lions** can be dangerous.* *∅ **Pens** used to have nibs.*
UNCOUNT	----------	----------	*∅ **Honesty** is the best policy.*

The articles for generic reference in particular take time to acquire. Have <u>∅ patience</u> in <u>the classroom.</u>

21.5 Unique reference

21.5.1 Proper names (proper nouns)

Names specify what is unique, so they don't require an article, but there are exceptions, especially with postmodification:

The London *she saw... **The Robert** she had known*

Some names have a built-in definite article, e.g. *The Hague, The Bronx, The Vatican,* etc.

21.5.2 Community unique / shared experience

The sun is unique enough for us, but not for astronomers or space travellers. When *the* is used with *parliament* the interlocuters are usually referring to the parliament in their country. Similarly but again in a smaller community with *the doctor, the butcher's, the bus stop,* etc, until we blend with the definite specific reference assumed from context, as in *we took the TV with us* in 21.2 above.

21.6 Other uses of the indefinite article

Uses like *He's **a** mechanic; it's **a** girl,* etc, may not be similar in other languages.

21.7 Other uses of the definite article

A type of generic use suits the following:

1. musical instruments (BrE): *Can you play the clarinet?*
2. media and places of entertainment: *the radio, the theatre, the cinema*
3. metonymy (part for the whole): *the Crown, the screen, the boards*
4. inventions: *the microchip, the TV, the pen*

Other fixed expressions and uniques are

5. comparatives and superlatives: *the faster of the two ... the fastest of them all*
6. adjectives as nouns: *the rich, the handicapped*
7. geographical names: *The Nile, The Himalayas*
8. most newspapers: *The Mirror, The Evening Echo*

21.8 Zero or *the* with institutions and everyday locations/activities

[1] *in hospital/prison : in the hospital/prison*   [2] *to/at work, church; to/in bed; at home,* etc.

The zero article in [1] connotes a stay while the definite article purely identifies the location (AmE prefers the definite article for both uses, though). The zero article in [2] seems again to focus more on the state or activity rather than the precise location (*at play* is pure state/activity). *Work* meaning place of work always takes the zero article and is preceded by a preposition or *leave,* etc.

The article is often omitted in abbreviated text in newspaper headlines, notes, etc.

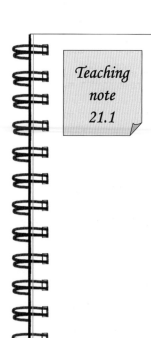

Teaching note 21.1

Japanese and other languages have very different systems of marking (a) nouns, so it's important to remember to speak (b) the articles clearly and include them on (c) the board.

(d) KIM'S GAME is an excellent way of presenting specific reference:

1. Take about 15 items one by one out of (e) a bag and check vocabulary, e.g. "What's this? Yes, it's *a* comb, very good, Yoshi." Or "Nobody? Well, it's *a* comb." Write *a comb*, not just *comb* on the board. Don't forget *a pair of scissors* etc, and even *some paper clips* etc, for variety. Put (f) the items where all can see, and ideally, touch.

2. When all the items are out, clean (g) the board and ask the students to try to remember them all.

3. Put the items back in the bag.

4. Ask (h) students to open a new page in their notebooks and write down as many of the items as they can remember (try it yourself also!).

5. Again take the items back out of the bag one by one and ask "Who forgot <u>the</u> clothes peg?" etc.

6. Reward the best student and discuss (i) memory power.

Task 21.1 | Identify the functions of the articles preceding the highlighted noun/-phrases above.

22 Discourse markers

22.1 Definition and word class

Discourse markers are cohesive devices, used mainly 1) to relate one sentence (or clause) to another, or 2) to signal the speaker's/writer's attitude or style. Without discourse markers we just have bare sentences, no discourse. Discourse markers are sometimes called *signposts*. The term *linkers* may also be used but this usually includes conjunctions (see chapter 16).

Discourse markers are **sentential adverbials**, i.e. they modify the whole sentence/clause. Sometimes they may even be clauses themselves. They have more to do with vocabulary than grammar; however, an introduction here is useful for reference purposes.

Task 22.1 Four of the discourse markers below have been mismatched. Identify and correctly rearrange them (this list is not exhaustive).

DISCOURSE MARKER (TEXTUAL)	FUNCTION/TYPE
1. *however, on the other hand, still, yet, nevertheless, at the same time, though*	a) alternative/contrastive
2. *in fact*	b) cause, result, transition
3. *as it happens, surprisingly, incidentally*	c) sequential
4. *after all, besides*	d) concessive – reasoning
5. *unfortunately, sadly, as luck would have it*	e) attitudinal
6. *first(ly), first of all, lastly*	f) enumerative
7. *therefore, hence, accordingly, so*	g) reinforcing, fuller detail
8. *frankly*	h) stylistic – truthful, dismissive
9. *then, next, afterwards, beforehand, finally*	i) coincidental, odd

22.2 Position

Most discourse markers can occur in initial, mid and end position, although some are restricted, e.g. *frankly, sorry* are usually restricted to initial position and *though, too* to end position.

Be careful with **however stressful** *the work may be,* etc, where *however* is not a discourse marker but an adverb modifying the adjective *stressful.*

22.3 Conversational discourse markers

The discourse markers above are **textual**: they usually appear in a flow of text or speech. Other discourse markers are used in conversation, i.e. when the (next) speaker indicates agreement, contradiction, indignation, etc. A few common ones are shown below. Intonation is important in conveying their meaning, in fact (!) *right, well* and *now* often act as 'intonation carriers' where the intonation can be more important than the word.

Some of these conversational discourse markers may also act as textual discourse markers so also appear above.

DISCOURSE MARKER (CONVERSATIONAL)	FUNCTION/TYPE
right	agreement, understanding, attention
now	staging, warning, result
at the same time	alternative/contrastive
well	reservation, thought, downplay
as a matter of fact	corrective, coincidental
actually	corrective, truth, surprising
I mean	indignation, emphasis
anyway	reverting to main topic

22.4 Punctuation

In simple sentences, generally a comma is used to separate the discourse marker from the rest of the sentence, but especially in initial position there is some flexibility and if a faster flow of text is required the comma may be omitted, but not at the expense of clarity, of course.

In longer sentences where a discourse marker modifies a second clause a comma at the end of the first clause may suffice (see the fourth sentence in 22.3). However, it is usually advisable to replace the comma by a semi-colon to indicate the primary break between clauses (see the last sentence in 22.1). With longer clauses and for more emphasis on the discourse marker a full stop may be called into service (see the preceding two sentences here).

Task 22.2

1. Explain the difference in meaning between the following:

    a) *first*   b) *firstly*   c) *at first*
  d) *at the end*   e) *in the end*   f) *at last*

2. Which two of the above are not discourse markers?

Task 22.3

In reply to the question *Is the exam done on paper?* a student says:
Actually the exam is done on paper but next year it will be done on computer.
What is the error here?

3 **Continue the following sentences in a logical way using both adverbs.**

a My aunt fell down the stairs the other day.
    Fortunately ...
    Obviously ...

b My dad's been on a strict diet for nearly a month now.
    Strangely ...
    Naturally ...

From *Cutting Edge Intermediate* by S. Cunningham & P. Moor (Pearson). Adverbs as discourse markers.

23 Negation

23.1 Form and use

To form a negative sentence in English we **negate the auxiliary verb**, i.e. we put the negative adverb *not* (often reduced to *n't*) after it:

>*She **could** wear high heels.*   *She **could not** (couldn't) wear high heels.*

If there is no auxiliary verb we insert **do**, *which is sometimes called the 'dummy' auxiliary*:

>*She **wears** high heels*   *She **does not** (doesn't) wear high heels.*

If the verb is **be** we negate that:

>*She **was** on the catwalk.*   *She **was not** (wasn't) on the catwalk.*

The negative adverb *never* can be used instead of *not*, occurring either side of the modals or *have/be*, but before *do* or the main verb.

>The contraction can alternate between *be/have* and *not*, with little if any semantic difference:

>>*He**'s not** listening ~ He **isn't** listening.*

Not (and *never*) can also negate other word classes:

>*Not Josephine, not blue, not running, never on a Sunday.*

23.2 Double negatives

Double negatives, e.g. **I didn't see nothing,* are sometimes transferred into English from the student's L1. English doesn't officially allow these but they are popular colloquially, especially in pop songs, often including the obliging *ain't* (for *haven't* (aux.) / *isn't*, etc.).

23.3 *No* and *none*

The negative determiner *no* means *not one/any* before countable, and *not any* before uncountable nouns. It carries a certain emphasis or air of finality:

>*I have **no** desire to discuss your verrucas.*

None is a pronoun when it stands for *no X*, the *X* being countable or uncountable:

>*They got plenty but I got **none** (no apples, no soup).*

None of + plural subject can take a singular (formal) or plural (informal) verb:

>*None of the guests has/have arrived yet.*

For *no one* see 7.6.

49.1 Complete the sentences with a word or phrase from (i) followed by a word or phrase from (ii). Use each word or phrase once only. (A–C)

(i)				(ii)		
no	~~none~~	none of		a drop	else	going to get
no-one	nothing	nowhere		heard	the hotels	~~in the cupboard~~
never	not			point	wrong	

1 Where are the biscuits? There's *none in the cupboard.*

2 We left the house as quietly as possible and .... us.

3 .... was spilt as she poured the liquid into the flask.

4 Jack was determined to leave and I knew that there was .... in protesting.

5 The door was locked and he had .... to go.

6 I found that .... in the city centre had any rooms left.

From *Advanced Grammar in Use* by M. Hewings (CUP). Negatives with *no, none*, etc.

24 Concord (agreement)

24.1 Person and number

In English the verb must agree with its subject in person (1st, 2nd, 3rd) and number (singular or plural). English verbs, however, are not inflected very much; in fact it is only the verb *be* which inflects for 1st, 2nd and 3rd) person (*am, are, is; was, were*). Other verbs apart from modals just add *-s* for the 3rd person singular, present tense. Modal auxiliaries don't inflect at all (although they do carry the tense); the primary auxiliaries *do* and *have* do (*does, has*).

24.2 *And* in coordination and apposition

We have seen plural and singular nouns and pronouns in previous chapters. We can also have coordinated subjects which will require a plural verb:

> *My brother and friend **are** here.*

However the coordination can sometimes be seen as singular:

> *Doom and gloom **was** all he spoke of.*

And be careful with [1] **apposition** and [2] **amounts**:

> [1] *My brother, and friend, **is** here.*   [2] *Twenty-five dollars **is** too much.*

24.3 *Either, neither* (with *or/nor*), *each, none*, etc.

There are two factors, among others, which have a bearing on the form of the verb following phrases containing these conjunctions/quantifiers/pronouns: 1) **proximity**, whereby whichever noun is closest to the verb can influence whether it will be plural or singular; 2) **notional concord**, where a noun or pronoun may be grammatically singular, but conveys a plural concept, thus allowing plural marking of the verb (see collective nouns, 5.2, for example).

Task 24.1

Fill in the blanks below with *have, has*, or *have/has* as appropriate.

1. *Either the house or the garden _____ to go.*
2. *Either the house or the gardens _____ to go.*
3. *Either the gardens or the house _____ to go.*
4. *Neither Zig nor Zag _____ been interviewed.*
5. *I don't think either of them _____ the guts for it.*
6. *Each of them, not counting the medics, _____ 200 rounds.*
7. *None of the guests _____ arrived yet.*
8. *A large number of problems _____ to be resolved.*
9. *The number of one-parent families seeking homes _____ risen.*

24.4 Subject-complement

Sometimes the subject is singular and the complement is plural, and vice versa. The verb is normally governed by the subject, but some flexibility is observable:

> *Low morals <u>are</u> his forte.*
> *What got sent in the end <u>was/were</u> daffodils.*

25 Genitive (possessive) case

25.1 Position

[1] *I don't have that company's tax returns.*
[2] *Governments love companies'/people's tax returns.*
[3] *Hans's lederhosen; Charles's plants.*
[4] *Cat Stevens' beard; Socrates' love of dialogue* (optionally pronounced with final /z1z/).
[5] *The girl in the yard's pencil case.*

The examples above show the positions of the *'s* (apostrophe *s*), what we commonly call **the possessive**, or the genitive case of the noun/-phrase.

Factors deciding the dropping of the *s* in [4] would appear to include one's time in history, but the number of syllables would have a stronger bearing.

25.2 *'s* or *of*

[1] *Clementine's sandals ; ?the sandals of Clementine*
[2] *John Lennon's songs ; the songs of John Lennon*
[3] *a dolphin's tail ; the tail of a dolphin*
[4] **a chair's leg ; the leg of a chair*
[5] *the water's edge ; the edge of the water*
[6] *a university's purpose ; the purpose of a university*
[7] *in two days' time ; *in the time of two days*
[8] *China's exports/cities ; the exports/cities of China*
[9] *?the theory's criticism ; the criticism of the theory*
[10] *for goodness' sake ; ?for the sake of goodness*

Task 25.1 Refer to the list above and fill in the blanks. The first three letters of the missing words are given to help you.

---

[1] to [4] show a change from human to (a) ina_____, with a corresponding shift from *'s* to *of*. Of course a chair doesn't have 'possessions' – what the *of* conveys is a part, hence we can have *the arm of a child* (or *a child's arm*, for animates), but not usually *the coat of a child*. Also with animates the *of* may indicate their (b) cre_____

[5] shows some literary (c) 'lic_____' to use the *'s*, perhaps with some personification.

[6], [7] and [8] show that three types of inanimate noun are quite comfortable with the *'s*:
(d) ins_____, time, and (e) pla_____.

[9] shows that the *'s* may cause (f) amb_____ regarding direction of effect.

[10] shows a common (g) exc_____, with little possessive meaning.

25.3 Other uses of the apostrophe
25.3.1 Contractions (short forms)
These are in the written form, reflecting the spoken form. The apostrophe indicates that one or more letters have been left out, e.g.

> *can't I'm you're they're there's it's we've*

Some forms are irregular, e.g. *won't, shan't*, and there are some spoken forms which are still not acceptable in written form, e.g. *there're, couldn't've*.

The dropping of weak vowels, syllables, etc, in speech is known as **elision**, e.g. (spoken) */remark'bly/*. Don't confuse with **ellipsis**, the leaving out of a word (see 16.2.1).

25.3.2 Plural of numbers, letters and words
As well as a creeping indiscriminate use of *it's* (see 7.2.1), what is known as the 'grocer's plural', e.g. **apple's, pear's*, etc, seems to be unavoidable in the streets.

What stymies the improving grocer, however, is the (correct) use of the apostrophe for the plural of numbers, letters, abbreviations and some words, e.g.

> *in the 60's (or 60s)   drop your h's   enough M.P.'s   too many* hence's

25.3.3 Shop and business names
The grocer's, the butcher's, the newsagent's, the doctor's, etc. Unfortunately, for language teachers at least, specialist shops are being replaced by the supermarket, with a consequent reduction in the legitimacy of much customer - shopkeeper role-play.

Apostrophes are the 'allmark of a Londoner.

26 Recognition test

Task 26.1 Match the bold parts of the sentences in the left column with their grammatical labels in the right column. Be careful - there are two redundant labels.

1. He **took over** when John was ill.	a) past participle	1. ___
2. She couldn't stop **worrying**.	b) infinitive	2. ___
3. **I'd think twice if I were you**.	c) -ing participle	3. ___
4. Where has he **gone**?	d) adverbial (preposition phrase)	4. ___
5. You can drive, **can't you**?	e) phrasal verb	5. ___
6. Would you like **to dance**?	f) tag question	6. ___
7. Mine is still trotting after **yours**.	g) gerund (-ing form)	7. ___
8. I don't know if I **do**.	h) first conditional	8. ___
9. The meeting**'s been postponed**.	i) second conditional	9. ___
10. He played his hand **like a pro**.	j) possessive independent pronoun	10. ___
11. The dog was chasing **its** tail.	k) possessive determiner pronoun	11. ___
12. Are you **talking** to me?	l) primary auxiliary verb	12. ___
	m) modal auxiliary verb	
	n) present perfect, passive	

Task 26.2 Instructions as for task 26.1 above.

13. The cat was licking **itself**.	a) -ing participle clause (reason)	13. ___
14. It **had been done** before.	b) adverb particle	14. ___
15. **If I'd known that I might've stayed**.	c) reported wh- question	15. ___
16. **Having come so far**, we wont' stop now.	d) definite article	16. ___
17. The show was **poorly** attended.	e) non-gradable adjective	17. ___
18. Don't go **unless** you're sure.	f) adverb of frequency	18. ___
19. Demand just dropped **off**.	g) identifying relative clause	19. ___
20. Clarke teed off **after the rain stopped**.	h) third conditional	20. ___
21. That's my eldest sister, **who lives in Goa**.	i) time clause	21. ___
22. Did Adrian wonder **what you did**?	j) non-identifying relative clause	22. ___
23. The bike **he had wanted** was a Harley.	k) past perfect, passive	23. ___
24. The concert was absolutely **brilliant**.	l) subordinator/conjunction	24. ___
	m) reflexive pronoun	
	n) adverb of degree – quantity	

Task 26.3 Instructions as for task 26.1 above.

25. She **must have known** all along.	a) superlative adjective	25. ___
26. We're **home**.	b) noun in genitive (possessive) case	26. ___
27. There's **somebody** prowling around.	c) adverb of place	27. ___
28. **In all honesty** I wouldn't have minded.	d) present continuous tense	28. ___
29. **They'll be closing** now.	e) discourse marker	29. ___
30. Not enough **fruit** is being eaten.	f) subject complement (adjective)	30. ___
31. It was **the most sensible** thing to do.	g) future continuous tense	31. ___
32. They didn't have **enough** cop-on.	h) quantifier (quantitive adjective)	32. ___
33. So **we're leaving** tomorrow.	i) indefinite pronoun – compound	33. ___
34. She crashed her **father's** car.	j) reported yes/no question	34. ___
35. James is **unwell**.	k) modal perfect of deduction	35. ___
36. **You** can never find one when you need one.	l) uncountable noun	36. ___
	m) collective noun	
	n) indefinite pronoun – generic *you*	

27 Error analysis and correction

27.1 What we must know about errors

A full analysis of student errors usually requires investigation of the causes of these, and is usually followed by suggestions for remedial teaching. Concerning the causes, many teachers, even without linguistic training or a command of the student's L1, can see or find out when an error is due to direct translation or overgeneralization of a known rule. More difficult to detect may be over-teaching of one form to the detriment of another, cross-cultural problems, avoidance strategies, etc.

The proportion of errors caused by L1 interference can range from about 30% to 65%, depending on the student's L1, i.e. the more the L1 resembles English the more the student will be inclined to use the syntax and lexis of their language, often falling into the trap of using what are known as 'false friends' in the process, e.g. *constipated* doesn't mean 'congested' (head cold) as *constipado* does in Spanish.

In language learning, errors are to a great extent manifestations of the student's progress along the learning path. Also keep in mind that some students like to experiment, making inevitable errors, while others prefer to wait until they are confident that what they produce will be correct.

On a point of terminology, the word *mistakes* in this field is reserved for slips of the pen or tongue, i.e. anything the student will self-correct if it is pointed out. *Errors*, on the other hand, are not readily recognised as such by their producers. In this chapter we also understand an error to be
1) spoken, 2) not part of the targeted language of the lesson in which it occurs, and 3) not above the production level of the student.

27.2 Correcting errors

It is as well to state here that many teachers do not believe in correcting. In truth there is not enough conclusive research evidence to justify prescriptive methods in this regard. Furthermore we each have our own way of correcting people when we are in conversation, and carry a preferred method into the classroom. On the part of the student, and this is the priority of course, again you will find mixed attitudes, but leaning towards more rather than less correction.

Leaving that aside, in your ELT training course you may be asked to design an on-the-spot error-correction technique, usually for a spoken error, small class, and presuming the other students would appreciate the mini-lesson also. A suggested procedure would be to follow a shortened version of the popular (if often criticized) *three P's* model (**p**resentation, controlled **p**ractice, free **p**ractice). Due to the descriptive detail involved in the following example its execution would seem to take some time, but actually no more than ten or fifteen minutes is recommended to be spent on this.

ERROR: *I no like cabbage.* (Level of class: elementary)

DESCRIPTION OF ERROR:

The rule for the formation of negative statements from affirmative ones which have no auxiliary verb and whose main verb is not *be* is: after the subject insert the auxiliary *do* (and adjust for tense) followed by the negative adverb *not*. These are usually contracted to *don't* (for third person singular read *does ... doesn't*). The student has not applied this rule.

CAUSE OF ERROR:

usually taken to be L1 interference, e.g. from Spanish:
> *No me gusta el repollo.* = *I don't like cabbage.*

CORRECTION (LESSON PLAN)

Presentation:

Presentation is the early stage of a lesson; it consists mainly of teacher-student interaction in feeding, eliciting, explaining and exemplifying targeted language.

1. Thank the student for her contribution and soft correct with, e.g. *So, you don't like cabbage, Christina. What about potatoes? And Paella? ... I love Paella too. You know what I <u>don't</u> like? ... I don't like garlic. Ugh. Onions are okay, but <u>I don't like</u> garlic* (draw garlic or translate if monolingual class).

2. Write the correct version on the board. Say the sentence at almost normal speed. Underline or otherwise highlight the relevant parts: *Christina <u>doesn't like</u> cabbage.* Under that add *I <u>don't like</u> garlic* (note that the referent for the 'I' on a board should be clear - hence the speech balloon).

3. Beside each sentence include a drawing to aid memory and add enjoyment. This allows further input, e.g. *Now here's Christina, pointing to some cabbage. She really doesn't like cabbage. No, sir!* Note: **don't be afraid to draw** - even if your attempts are awful it's always fun and encourages participation. Chat and elicit vocab, spelling, etc, from students while drawing.

4. Elicit another example for the board from a student. *What about sports, hobbies? Seung, do you like fishing?* If Seung just says 'No' or 'Yes' accept this. *Ah, so you like fishing, that's nice. I'm afraid I don't; I fall asleep. What about football, tennis, skiing?* Now Seung cannot just say 'no' or 'yes'. Write the third model sentence on the board, with a drawing. This can be positive rather than negative, for comparison: *Seung likes fishing.*

Figure 5. Board work for presentation and controlled practice of *don't like.*

Controlled practice:

Controlled practice is generally understood to consist mainly of repetition of phrases/sentences containing the targeted language, with hard correction (hard correction is where you point out that an error has been made, clearly 'model' the phrase and ask for another effort).

How much drilling is done largely depends on the students and their needs. Some nationalities and age groups like 'sing-song' choral repetition; others find it strange. For these latter controlled practice usually means intensive practice in the form of gap-filling or matching etc, individual or collaborative, followed by checking around and hard correcting any serious errors. Your coursebook or resource book would provide these types of exercises for most grammar points.

For this class we will imagine learners who enjoy choral repetition and whose pronunciation would benefit from same:

Controlled practice (contd.):

1. Model (say "Listen", and pronounce clearly) *She doesn't like cabbage,* indicating stress pattern by gesturing or tapping on the desk/board. Also point to the relevant drawing. Ask students to repeat as you 'conduct' – it is important that they keep together. Repeat once more, hard correcting where appropriate Finally, ask for one or two individual repetitions. Accept any decent effort and move on.
2. Do likewise with the other sentences on the board.
3. Elicit a different like/dislike sentence to add variety, and treat in the same way.

Free practice:

Free practice generally means students genuinely conversing with each other without interruption from the teacher. Role-play/drama also goes under this heading. Some writing may be included.

1. Specify/elicit about 3 topics and write them on the board, e.g. *food, sports, animals*.
2. Students in pairs. A asks two questions (*What food do you like? What food do you not like?*). B answers, then it's B's turn to ask A. Then both students write down the answers they got in one sentence containing two clauses, e.g. *Fidel likes carrots but he doesn't like peas.*
3. N.B. The pairwork should first be demonstrated by the teacher with a good student.
4. When more than half of the students have finished, stop the pair work.
5. Ask for a few sentences and write some on the board. Comment briefly and thank all students.

Alternative pairwork:

1. Individually, students write down what they like and don't like – topics on the board.
2. Student A asks student B to guess the liked/disliked item, within 3 guesses. Clues should be given. Score a point if student B can't guess. Then alternate. One could be false for a 'call my bluff' variation.
3. As points 4 and 5 above, but also ask about and comment on some scores.

Role-play as an alternative to question-and-answer pairwork:

1. Allot roles and scenarios that would elicit *like* and *don't like*. One suggestion would be a jobshop interview where the candidate is not too keen on what's on offer; or mother and teenage daughter in a clothing store, the mother trying to buy 'sensible' clothes for her daughter.
2. Demo a short related role-play with a good student.
3. Ask pairs to write brief notes rather than a full script for their role-play. Groups of three might also be suitable. Remind students to include *like* and *don't like* in the script, and to keep it short, about four turns each. Encourage some kind of conflict resolution/denouement in the role-play.
4. Some fun can now be had as each pair (or as many as time or tolerance allows) acts out their script.
5. Check that the correct form has been reinforced and thank all students.

Task 27.1 Identify the 'error' in the cartoon above (use grammatical terminology).

Task 27.2 The sentences below contain errors made by ESOL students. Define the errors accurately, always using grammatical terms. The first one has been done for you.

0. I don't know what will I do.
   No inversion required in reported question.

1. In war, many people die and many buildings destroy.

2. We went downtown for seeing a movie.

3. He hasn't got some wine.

4. Where you go last night?

5. You should to eat better food.

6. Klaus has come to visit me last week.

7. Sometimes I'm going to the shops.

8. There's nothing to do, so I'm very boring.

9. I want to avoid the mistakes who the teachers made before.

10. He buyed a new car last year.

11. She is going to give up to smoke.

12. One of the modules is Spanish Grammar's Practical Teaching.

13. They need believe in something.

14. How many furniture do you want?

15. He said me that the class was finished.

16. We asked her if she can bring Jim Morrison back to life.

17. We went back to home.

18. After a flight of two hours – most of it we spent studying – we landed in Gdansk.

19. The life is very hard there.

20. My first reaction was to shout, but after I thought this was not a good idea.

APPENDIX - LEVEL GUIDELINES

This table comprises mainly the grammatical contents of some popular coursebooks. The order of items within the levels is not fixed. Items may be taught at a previous level depending on the coursebook used or learners' requirements and aptitudes. Learners can understand but not produce many higher level items.

BEGINNER	ELEMENTARY	PRE-INTERMEDIATE	INTERMEDIATE	UPR. INTERMEDIATE	ADVANCED
Greetings, introductions (personal pronouns + be)	Polite requests, offers and refusals	Present perfect simple	Present perfect continuous; time preps. *since* and *for*	Verb + gerund or infinitive, e.g. *remember writing; remember to write*	Recycle relative clauses, incl. with prep. + rel. pronoun
Articles *a/the* (non-generic ref.)	Likes/dislikes	Making suggestions	Modal probability/deduction (present and past) e.g. *must/could be, must/could have done*	3rd conditional	Verb + obj. + infinitive(/-ing), e.g. *make him go; force him to go; saw him go/going*
Jobs, nationalities	Modals *can + have to*	Modals of perm., oblig., ability	2nd conditional	Recycle modal perfects, incl. *needn't have*	Recycle 3rd conditional, incl. inversion. Mixed conditionals
What + be questions (pres.)	Past simple of common regular and irregular verbs	Time clauses	*Is like, looks like*	*I wish* + past, past perfect	Inversion after negative adverbial, e.g. *Seldom had I seen ...*
(Alphabet)	Past continuous	Zero and 1st conditional (+ 2nd)	Reciprocal & reflexive pronouns	Future perfect	Cleft sentences
Days, months, seasons	Wh- questions (simple)	Apologising, inviting, ordering, advising	Recycle defining rel. clause	Non-defining relative clause	Participle clauses
Colours, numbers, time	Yes/no questions with 'do'	Indefinite pronouns, compound *some/anyone/body, no/everybody*	Basic phrasal verbs	Recycle phrasal verbs, incl. 3-word types	Preparatory 'it', e.g. *It surprises me that...*
Giving directions (*Where + be* questions (pres.))	Descriptive adjectives	Defining relative clause	Recycle future forms	Passive – perfect, future & continuous. + with *get*	Passive – infinitive, + with ditransitive verbs
There is/are, + question and negative form	Comparative and superlative form	Recycle question forms, incl. yes/no type with modals	Quantifiers *little/few*	Correlative conjunctions, e.g. *either ... or*	Present subjunctive, e.g. *if need be*
Quantifiers *some/any*	Quantifiers *many/much, a little/a few, enough*	Passive – present simple (+ past)	-ing adjs. & past participial adjs.	*Be used to* + gerund	Ellipsis
Basic countable and uncountable nouns (food)	Basic adverbs of manner	Recycle future forms, incl. pres. cont. for arrangement	Passive – present and past	Causative, e.g. *Have/make John repair it*	Complex discourse markers
Basic prepositions	Basic prepositions	Adverbs *already* and *yet;* basic quantity adverbs	Question tags	Phrasal modals, e.g. *had better, would rather*	Compound adjectives
Present continuous	Present continuous	Basic conjunctions and link words	Stative verbs	Further discourse markers	'That' clauses, e.g. *the fact/news that ...*
Present simple	Present simple	Pro-form *so*, e.g. *I think so*	Pro-form *not*, e.g. *I hope not*	Infinitive of purpose, e.g. *I went there to buy a paper*	Adverb + verb collocation, e.g. *categorically deny*
Possessive *'s* + poss. adjs.	Semi-modal *have to*	Comparative *as X as*	Basic discourse markers	*As* vs. *like; such a* vs. *so*	Recycle phrasal modals, incl. *be to, be apt to,* etc.
Sports/leisure, parts of body	Time phrases and clauses, e.g. *when I arrived*	*Used to* (past habit or state)	Non-gradable adjectives	Common idioms	Formulae & expressions, e.g. *More's the pity, bored stiff*
House rooms & furniture	*Whose*. Possessive pronouns	Reported statements and commands	*Would* for past habit	*Say/tell*	
Demonstrative adjectives	Degree adverbs *too, very*	Instructions (e.g. for recipes), with indefinite pro., generic *you*	Reported questions	Verb + obj + prep. e.g. *accuse sbdy of*	
Place adverbs *here, there*	Basic frequency adverbs	Clothing, pair nouns	Pro-forms: *So/neither do I*		
Modal *can/can't*	Reflexive pronouns (sing.)		Verb/adj + prep. e.g. *insist on, jealous of*		
Would like + noun/-phrase (requests)	Ordinal numbers, dates		Past perfect		
	Personality adjectives, job & routine activity vocab.		Partitives, *each of, most of,* etc.		

KEY TO TASKS

Some of the tasks in table format are reproduced here in the same format; others are not. This is decided by perceived benefit and availability of space.

1.1
sloop (noun only)   *rile* (verb only)

1.2

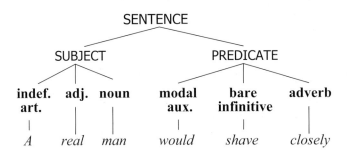

1.3
1. Adjectives usually go before (premodify) the noun. Postmodification may occur if there is a comma and a longer phrase, e.g. *like a jewel, very precious yet sometimes neglected.*
2. Adjectives are not inflected; there is no plural adjective form in English.
3. The personal pronoun of the subject may not follow it immediately (but the reflexive pronoun may), i.e. subjects are not repeated, except in apposition or for stylistic reasons, in which case a comma would be required.
4. An English sentence/clause with a finite verb requires a subject. For exceptions see *ellipsis*.

1.4
1. a) noun b) -ing participle
2. a) modal aux. verb b) definite article
3. a) *be* as aux. verb b) pronoun
4. a) bare infinitive b) adverb
5. a) pronoun b) adjective
6. a) noun b) -ing participle
7. a) verb b) adjective
8. a) noun b) modal aux. verb
9. a) modal aux. verb b) bare infinitive
10. a) indefinite article b) adverb

1.5
(There is also scope for designing this activity without the prepositions, e.g. *Do you leave your shoes ……………?*)
Possible questions and completions:
1. *At night, do you leave your shoes under (the bed)?*
2. *Do you cook vegetables in (a wok)?*
3. *Are there any pictures on (the wall in your kitchen)?*
4. *Is there any shampoo on (the shelf in your bathroom)?*
5. *What is on top of (the Eiffel Tower)?*
6. *What is in front of (your house)?*
7. *What is opposite (your house)?*
8. *Do you work in (a factory)?*
9. *What was your favourite subject at (school)?*
10. *What is the name of the city between (Sidney and Melbourne)?*

1.6
A preposition must be followed by a noun/-phrase or pronoun. The word *to* in *look forward to* is a preposition, not part of the infinitive, evidenced by the noun following it in, for example, *look forward to summer*. A noun is therefore required – in this case an -ing form used as a noun (gerund) – instead of the infinitive particle *see*.

1.7

Note: You are not expected to know the student's language but to guess the causal elements.

1 * *I think I was member of this family.* (Japanese L1)
  a) I think I was <u>a</u> member of this family.
  b) Omission of indefinite article where unknown or non-unique reference requires it.
  c) Perhaps there is no indefinite article in Japanese.

2. **The sports ground is in a town at the sea.* (Arabic L1)
  a) The sports ground is in a town <u>by</u> the sea
  b) Incorrect preposition. (Missing the target *on the coast* also a possibility, but no room for further discussion here.)
  c) Perhaps there is one preposition in Arabic that covers the semantic range of English *at* and *by*.

3. * *...I could feel the soft rain in my face.* (Spanish L1)
  a) I could feel the soft rain <u>on</u> my face.
  b) Incorrect preposition.
  c) In Spanish perhaps there is one preposition that covers the semantic range of English *in* and *on*.

4. **I have never been in Mars.* (Spanish L1)
  a) I have never been <u>to</u> Mars.
  a) Incorrect preposition.
  b) In Spanish the preposition corresponding to the English *to* is not used with *been* to mean 'visit'.

5. **I came back willinglessly.* (Chinese L1)
  a) I came back <u>unwillingly</u>.
  a) Incorrect adverb of manner..
  b) The student is overgeneralising from *hopelessly* etc. No influence from Chinese is perceived.

6. **I thought maybe I could found some animals there.* (Spanish L1)
  a) I thought maybe I could <u>find</u> some animals there.
  b) The modal aux. verb must be followed by the bare infinitive.
  c) Perhaps just a lapse in concentration, or missed target *could have found*, as the level is apparently not low. (Spanish uses its infinitive after a modal aux.)

1.8

1. a) *be* as aux. verb   b) preposition   6. a) modal aux. verb   b) -ing participle
2. a) noun   b) gerund (/-ing form as noun)   7. a) linking verb (in bare infin. form) b) noun
3. a) *be* as aux. verb   b) pronoun   8. a)adverb   b) adjective
4. a) linking verb   b) adjective   9. a) linking verb   b) preposition
5. a) definite article   b) gerund (/-ing form as noun)   10. a) pronoun   b) bare infin. (main verb)

2.1   **2.2**   **2.3**
1b   2e   5a   1e   3a   5c   3d   4e   5c

2.4

1. future continuous   2. present continuous   3. past simple   4. present simple   5. past continuous
6. future simple

2.5

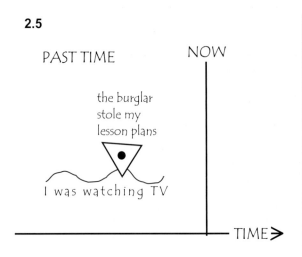

3.1   1.

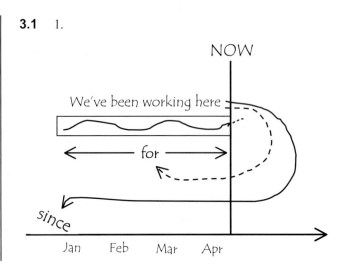

3.1 (contd.)

2. (a) prepositions   (b) *For*   (c) *since*   (d) *for*

3.2

1. *I'll be with you now.*	*future simple*
2. *I want it yesterday.*	*present simple*
3. *He's seen the light.*	*present perfect simple*
4. *Are you joking?*	*present continuous*
5. *I wanted to know your name.*	*past simple*
6. *You've been trying that all night.*	*present perfect continuous*
7. *She'll be going up the wall.*	*future continuous*
8. *You weren't really listening.*	*past continuous*

3.3

1. *I hadn't been abroad before that.*	*past perfect simple*
2. *He had a cold.*	*past simple*
3. *Has he been bothering you?*	*present perfect continuous*
4. *They've had the boat 3 years now.*	*present perfect simple*
5. *She'd been wondering about the price.*	*past perfect continuous*

3.4

1. you'll (probably) have been studying 2. You'll have been using   3. you will have bought
4. You will (possibly also) have read   5. you'll have made 6. you will have been invited

4.1

1. *I'm out* and *I've got*: pres simple for timetables.   2. *I'm visiting*: pres. continuous for arrangements.
3. *I'm not going to make it* and *It's going to be longer*: 'obvious' future.
4. *Shall we?*: suggestion.   5. *I'll just check*: offer   6. *I'll confirm that*: promise
(Is two o'clock OK? could be present simple for future, depending on the meaning, e.g. *I've got nothing in the afternoon* could also mean *nothing in my diary,* present time.)
For *can* with future reference see task 13.1.

4.2

1. *What will your Ma say?*	*future simple*
2. *She'd waited as long as possible.*	*past perfect simple*
3. *Have you been clubbing in the caves?*	*present perfect continuous*
4. *They'll have taken everything by then.*	*future perfect simple*
5. *I did everything I could.*	*past simple*
6. *They'd been preparing to leave.*	*past perfect continuous*
7. *I was looking to see if she was looking.*	*past continuous*
8. *Sally's gone back to her roots.*	*present perfect simple*
9. *How's it going?*	*present continuous*
10. *How long will they have been driving?*	*future perfect continuous*

4.3

TENSE	EXAMPLE	USE
1. present simple	f) *You just never listen, do you?*	vii) regular/habitual event, fact
2. present continuous	k) *She's standing her ground.*	ix) happening now (temporary)
3. past simple	g) *Neil stepped down.*	xiii) completed past event
4. past continuous	e) *I was just looking at it.*	xi) 'background' past event
5. future simple	a) *It'll be alright on the night.*	v) prediction of completed event
6. future continuous	h) *Bill will be seeing his secretary Monday.*	iv) prediction of 'simultaneous' event /happening as a matter of course
7. 'going to' future	m) *You're not going to watch Star Wars again, are you?*	i) plan
8. present perfect simple	j) *That's torn it.*	viii) recent event or life experience
9. present perfect cont.	i) *How long have you been telling that joke?*	xii) continuous up to now
10. past perfect simple	c) *The plant had grown a foot in our absence.*	x) completed event before main past reference
11. past perfect cont.	b) *We'd been trying to get it started.*	vi) continuous before main past reference
12. future perfect simple	l) *They'll have destroyed half the rainforests by 2020.*	ii) predicted to have happened by a future time
13. future perfect cont.	d) *They'll have been talking for ten hours come midnight.*	iii) continuous action up to a future time (duration stated)

4.4

In this case it's really the adjective *cold* that has a stative or dynamic meaning, linked with *be*. If it refers to temperature/sensation then the sentence is unacceptable because with that sense *be* is also stative and may not be used in the continuous aspect. If *cold* means *unfriendly*, in fact showing unfriendliness through some *activity*, then *be* is dynamic and is correctly used in the continuous aspect.

4.5

Typically (with durative verbs) the perfect simple conveys finality or achievement, e.g. in [1] the speaker may well be about to move house. It is also often used to focus on the person rather than the activity.

The perfect continuous, on the other hand, is more often employed for focussing on the duration and the activity itself, and implies future continuity.

4.6

1) The past continuous has been used erroneously; there is no simultaneous or background event so the past simple is required. The student's L1 would appear to have an imperfect tense, which the student thinks approximates to the past continuous in English.

2) *After* is a preposition and therefore must be followed by a noun/phrase, or in this case a gerund (-ing form used as a noun), *finishing*. (*After* could also be a conjunction in a time clause, e.g. *after I finished my studies*.)

5.1

1. (suggested) We'll need a few <u>cakes</u> for the party.　　Would you like some more <u>cake</u>?

2. people

6.1

Less is primarily used with uncount nouns, e.g. *less air, less friction,* but it is also acceptable with count nouns, e.g. *less people, less students,* in informal registers. *Fewer* is used only with count nouns and when a more formal register is required, e.g. *fewer people, fewer students*.

7.1

The subject case is often preferred after the preposition b*etween*, to lend an air of 'correctness' or formality: *between you and I* instead of *between you and me* (even *between she and I*, etc.). Both are acceptable, although technically a preposition must be followed by the <u>object</u> case of the pronoun(s).

7.2

It is the dummy subject for *weather* in *It's very cold.* Other referents are distance, e.g. *It's 50 kilometres to the next petrol station,* and situation, e.g. *It's great/horrible here.*

7.3

The personal pronoun *it,* in *it's a shame* normally has forward reference, e.g. it refers to the noun clause *the way she makes me scrub the* floor in **It*'s a shame **the way she makes me scrub the floor**. It is therefore called the Preparatory Subject or Anticipatory Subject when it functions in this way. The demonstrative pronoun *that* usually has back reference, e.g. it refers to *She made me scrub the floor* in **"She made me scrub the floor."** "Really? **That**'s a shame."

When *it* refers to a noun/-phrase it usually has back reference, e.g. "I hope you like **the cake**. I made **it** myself."

7.4

a) *He:* personal　　*himself:* reflexive

c) *Everyone:* indefinite (compound)　　*their:* possessive determiner (possessive adjective)

d) *They:* personal　　*their:* possessive det. (poss. adj.)　　*each other:* reciprocal

8.1

1.

	SIZE	QUALITY	COLOUR	NATIONALITY	MATERIAL	PURPOSE	
A	big	old	red	Victorian	ceramic	water	jug

2. The macro types *qualitative* and *classifying* could be loosely spread, the former from SIZE to COLOUR and the latter from NATIONALITY to PURPOSE.

9.1

1. *Cowardly* is usually an adjective only. *He ran in a cowardly way* would be more acceptable.

9.2

[1]ALSO: focusing   [2]BADLY: manner/degree (quantity)   [3]WELL: manner/degree (quantity)
[4]OFTEN: frequency   [5]EASILY: manner   [6]DEFINITELY: manner/focusing   [7]LATE: time
[8]FAST: manner   [9]PERFECTLY: manner/degree (quantity)   [10]NEARLY: degree (quantity)
[11]DAILY: definite frequency   [12]GENTLY: manner   [13]ALWAYS: frequency
[14]SIMPLY: focusing/manner/maximizer   [15]NEVER: frequency/negative
[16]REALLY: intensifier/maximizer   [17]COMPLETELY: degree (quantity)
[18]HARDLY: broad negative/degree (quantity)   [19]ANGRILY: manner   [20]ONLY: focusing

10.1

(a) formal   (b) *farther*   (c) *further*   (d) *so*   (e) *extent/degree*   (f) adverb   (g) intensifier

11.1

TENSE (etc.)	ACTIVE	PASSIVE
present simple	*She takes photos.*	*Photos are taken by her.*
present continuous	*She is taking photos.*	*Photos are being taken by her.*
past simple	*She took a photo.*	*A photo was taken by her.*
past continuous	*She was taking a photo.*	*A photo was being taken by her.*
future simple	*She'll take a photo.*	*A photo will be taken by her.*
future with *going to*	*She's going to take a photo.*	*A photo is going to be taken by her.*
(future continuous)	*She'll be taking photos.*	*Photos will be being taken by her. [R]*
present perfect simple	*She has taken a decision.*	*A decision has been taken by her.*
(present perfect cont.)	*She has been taking photos.*	*Photos have been being taken by her. [R]*
past perfect simple	*She had taken photos before then.*	*Photos had been taken by her before then.*
future perfect simple	*She will have mastered relative clauses by next week.*	*Relative clauses will have been mastered by her by next week.*
modal	*Someone might buy it.*	*It might be bought.*
modal perfect	*Someone could have killed us.*	*We could have been killed.*
infinitive (or gerund)	*Someone needs to clean my desk.*	*My desk needs to be cleaned.* (or *My desk needs cleaning.* – only with *need, deserve, require, want*)
perfect infinitive	*Better to have loved.*	*Better to have been loved.*
gerund (of *be*)	*He doesn't like <u>it when someone tells him what to do</u>.*	*He doesn't like being told what to do.*

The [R] signifies that the future continuous and the continuous perfects are very rarely used in the passive.

11.2

a) 6   b) 5   c) 2   d) 3   e) 7   f) 4 The subject does the action. This is not causative but 'completive'.

11.3

(**About the meeting wasn't told to me.*) *About the meeting* is not an object but an adverbial. The sentence **They didn't tell about the meeting to me* is ungrammatical. *They didn't tell the news* (object) *to me* would be okay, allowing the transformation *The news wasn't told to me.*
The transformation of number 7 would be unacceptable because of the reduced clause *(what to do)*:
(**Has <u>what to do</u> been shown to you?*). There would be a little less awkwardness with *Has <u>what you are to do</u> been shown to you?* but the acceptability is still low.

13.1

can('t):	1c	2a	3b	4e	5d
could(n't):	1c	2b	3d	4e	5a
may (not):	1b	2c	3a	4d	
might(n't):	1a	2c	3b		
would(n't):	1b	2d	3c	4a	5e
should(n't):	1b	2c	3e	4a	5d
ought(n't) to:	1b	2c	3a		
must(n't):	1d	2c	3e	4a	5b

13.2

1. Here *need* is a main (lexical) verb and therefore cannot carry a negating suffix.

2. The general (non-) requirement is conveyed by the main verb *need* in b) *You don't need to lock your car.* A suggested following sentence is *There's almost no theft in Saudi Arabia.*
The more immediate or temporary non-requirement is expressed by the semi-modal *need* in b) *You needn't lock your car.* A following sentence might be *I'll be here until you come back.*

13.3

a) durative state in the past
b) habitual action in the past

13.4

1. must (internal obligation)
2. mustn't (command/strong obligation)
3. don't have to (no (external) obligation)
4. have to (external oblign.)
5. must (firm recommendation)
6. mustn't (command/ strong oblign.)
7. must (internal oblign.)
8. must (internal oblign.)

14.1

The object of this transitive phrasal verb may go between the verb + adverb. It may also go after the verb + adverb, but only in its full form, not as a pronoun.

14.2

1. The phrasal verb in b) is intransitive.
2. *See through* changes its meaning when the object *it* comes between the verb and the particle.
3. Sentence c).

15.1

6 g   7 f

15.2

1. Type 5 (wh- word as subject)   2. *Who. How goes the work?* etc, is possible but *how* and the other wh- words are adverbs so could not function as the subject, unlike *what* or *who*, being pronouns here.

16.1

5 g   7 e   11 l   12 k

18.1

1 & 2 a   3 & 8 c   4 & 9 e
5 d   6 & 7 b

18.2

(a) main   (b) intonation/tone
(c) *that*   (d) *whom*

18.3

a) 1	b) 2	c) 2	d) 1
e) 2	f) 1	g) 1	h) 2

18.4

1. *identified as the main suspect*: reduced relative clause (with past participle).
2. *speaking on television last night*: -ing participle clause (adverbial – time).
3. *that the man was dangerous and anyone seeing him should keep their distance*: reported speech clause(s).
5. *seeing him*: reduced relative clause (with -ing participle).
(Arguably, 2. could also be a reduced relative clause, but non-identifying. However, this does not seem to be discussed in most grammars. The fact that it can be fronted may deem it ineligible.)

18.5

1 d   2 a   3 f   4 h   5 c   6 e   7 b   8 g

19.1

(a) *future*   (b) *will*   (c) comma   (d) *if*   (e) slight/slim   (f) register   (g) imperative

19.2

(a) unreal/untrue/impossible/hypothetical   (b) improbable   (c) person   (d) subjunctive   (e) *should*
(f) *was*   (g) *were*   (h) *were*   (i) request

19.3

(a) contracted/short   (b) auxiliary (primary auxiliary)   (c) authentic/real/genuine

19.4

2 If the world's population <u>continues</u> to increase, we <u>will need</u> more food. 1ST COND.

3 If other intelligent beings <u>inhabited</u> the universe, they <u>would be</u> very different from us. 2ND COND.

4 If there <u>were</u> more TV programmes about science, people <u>would know</u> more about it. 2ND COND.

5 If we <u>had spent</u> less on space research, we <u>could have solved</u> many other serious problems. 3RD COND.

19.5

1. If this clause had a past perfect tense …	it would be able to form the 'if' clause of a 3rd conditional sentence. But we now have a 2nd conditional.	c)
2. If this clause had had a past simple tense …	it could have formed the 'if' clause of a 2nd conditional sentence. But now the sentence is a 3rd conditional.	f)
3. Unless you show me the right clause …	we will be here all day looking for this 1st conditional.	d)
4. If I found my partner easily …	it was because the zero conditional was obvious.	a)
5. If we hadn't looked at this carefully …	we mightn't have formed a 3rd conditional.	h)
6. If this clause were in the present tense …	it would be able to help form a 1st conditional. Instead we now have a 2nd conditional	g)
7. If we had studied the conditionals more …	we wouldn't be having so much trouble with this 'combo' 3rd & 2nd conditional.	b)
8. If I show this to the right person …	they will help me form a 1st conditional.	i)
9. If *whenever* can be substituted for *if* …	that sentence is usually a zero conditional.	e)

20.1

(a) infinitive   (b) infinitive   (c) -ing form
(d) -ing forms   (e) -ing form   (f) infinitive
(g) -ing form   (h) infinitive   (i) -ing form

20.2

a) FI   b) FI   c) E   d) FI e) BI   f) BI
g) FI   h) FI

21.1

(a) (Ø) unspecific   (b) unique   (c) general knowledge/context   (d) (Ø) unique, proper name
(e) unspecific   (f) previously mentioned (definite specific)   (g) as (f)
(h) article omitted for abbreviation (previously mentioned)   (i) (Ø) generic (uncountable)

22.1

2 g   3 i   7 b   9 c

22.2

a) *first* usually marks the first in a series of instructions or events.

b) *firstly* usually marks the first in a series of reasons.

c) *at first* indicates that there is a change to come later.

d) *at the end* usually refers to position in a line, time etc, opposite to *at the front/start*. It is therefore not a discourse marker but (part of) a preposition group, e.g. *He waited <u>at the end of</u> the line/gets paid <u>at the end of</u> the month*.

e) *in the end* marks how a story ends, sometimes ironically.

f) *at last* implies some impatience, the awaited being overdue. It is entered in the dictionary as an idiom, not an adverbial. It also does not act as a cohesive device or attitude signaller to any great extent, so it is not a discourse marker.

22.3

'Actually' is a false friend translated from Romance languages where its counterpart (e.g. Spanish *actualmente)* means 'at present', 'currently', etc. ('At present' and 'currently' are usually called time adverbials.)

24.1

1. has/have (*have* is often regarded as 'incorrect' but is acceptable in informal registers)   2. *have.*
3. *have* (contradicting the proximity rule, the plural generally wins here)   4. *have/has* (as 1, but there is also a notional plurality provided by the concept 'both Zig and Zag were omitted')
5. *have/has* (as 4, but also proximity with *them*)   6. *has* (*each* always singular)
7. *has/have* (see 23.3)   8. *have* (similar to *a lot of,* 6.3)   9. *has* (definite singular subject)

25.1

(a) inanimate   (b) creations   (c) licence   (d) institutions   (e) places   (f) ambiguity   (g) exclamation

26.1

					T26.2				T26.3			
1 e	2 g	3 i	4 a	5 f	13 m	14 k	15 h	16 a	25 k	26 c	27 i	28 e
6 b	7 j	8 l	9 n	10 d	17 n	18 l	19 b	20 i	29 g	30 l	31 a	32 h
11 k	12 c				21 j	22 c	23 g	24 e	33 d	34 b	35 f	36 n

27.1

The father means 'How much money', where *much* is a quantifier (quantitive adjective) modifying the noun *money* understood (or *much* is a quantifying pronoun, standing for *much money*). The son interprets *much* as an adverb of degree (quantity), modifying the verb *want.*

27.2

(Chapter numbers where the point is dealt with follow the error definitions below.)
1. Passive voice required when the object of the action comes before the verb (11.1).
2. *For* + -ing form used instead of infinitive of purpose (20.3).
3. The quantifier *some* is used in affirmative sentences, *any* in questions and negatives (6.6).
4. The aux. verb *do* is required to form a question if there is no other auxiliary or the verb *be* in use (15).
5. A modal auxiliary verb should be followed by a bare infinitive (1.4).
6. *Come* should be in the past tense (not present perfect), as a past time has been mentioned (3.1) (& teaching note 3.1).
7. Present simple required for habitual actions (2.1).
8. Past participial instead of -ing participial adjective required, as this describes the person's feelings (8.3) (& teaching note 8.1).
9. Relative pronoun for things is *that* or *which* (18.2).
10. Overgeneralisation, treating an irregular verb as regular. Past tense is *bought* (12).
11. The transitive phrasal verb *give up* doesn't take an infinitive as object (perhaps because the 'tentative/future' property of the infinitive conflicts with the 'fulfilment' property of *give up*) (task 20.1).
12. *Grammar* is inanimate so the *of* possessive should be used (25.2, see numbers 4 and 9 in the list).
13. *Need* as a modal is generally used only in the negative or interrogative (13.7.1). Otherwise when it functions as a main verb it is followed by the full infinitive.
14. *Furniture* is an uncountable noun, so the quantifier *much* must be used (6.2).
15. *Said* does not take a personal object (17.6).
16. Back-shift rule should be implemented in most past time reported speech (17.2).
17. *Home* is an adverb of direction in this case, not a noun requiring a preposition of direction (9.2).
18. Relative pronoun *which* required in non-identifying relative clause (18.3).
19. Generic reference with uncountable nouns requires zero article (21.4).
20. *After* usually serves as a preposition; a sequential discourse marker is required here. Choice of *then, later, afterwards,* etc. (22.1).

BLANK PAGE

INDEX

Reference is generally to chapter (and section), sometimes to a task.